Joe's whole name was Joseph-Simon-Bar Jason.
He was named Joseph after one uncle and Simon
after another uncle, and Bar meant he was the son
of his father Jason. A name like that could make
you stoop-shouldered carrying it around. It was
much quicker to call him Joe.

Joe lived in Jerusalem with his grandmother,
in a small house snuggled against the city wall
on the other side of town. When Joe's grandmother got the feeling that something special was
going to happen, her bones twanged and she said,
"I feel it in my bones." And when grandmother's
bones twanged, something always happened. Joe
could count on it.

Six days before Passover, grandmother's bones
began twanging. "Something's going to happen this
week," she said. "I just feel it in my bones."

Joe and his friend Andy rushed out into the
crowded streets to find out what had set grandmother's bones twanging. Something special
happened all right!

It changed Joe's life and all of history.

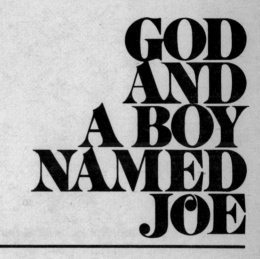

# GOD AND A BOY NAMED JOE

Ethel Barrett

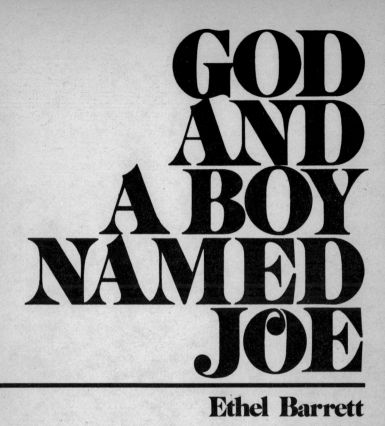

A Regal Venture Book
A Division of G/L Publications
Glendale, California, U.S.A.

The Scripture versions used in *God and a Boy Named Joe*
are from *The Living Bible,* Paraphrased (Wheaton:
Tyndale House, Publishers, 1971). Used by permission.

Second Printing, 1975
Third Printing, 1976

Published by
Regal Books Division, G/L Publications
Glendale, California 91209, U.S.A.

Library of Congress Catalog Card No. 74-16957
ISBN 0-8307-0324-1

# CONTENTS

# Chapter One

# FRIDAY

Grandmother's bones were twanging again.

She had said so, only this morning.

Joe thought about it as he plowed through the crowded Jerusalem street. When Grandmother's bones twanged, you'd better duck. Something always happened.

"Grandmother's bones are twanging again." He said it aloud to Andy, who was plowing along with him.

"Twanging?" puffed Andy. "What do you mean, twanging?"

"Well, it isn't that, really. They don't really *twang*. It's just that when she gets the feeling that something special is going to happen, she says, 'I feel it in my bones.'"

"Oh. You made her sound like a ten-stringed lyre."[1]

They stopped short in the crowd, and a donkey just behind them almost climbed up their backs.

"I tease her about it," Joe went on, as he pushed the donkey's nose to one side. "I call it twanging. It makes her laugh."

---

1. Rhymes with wire. It's like a small harp and you pluck it like a guitar.

1

"You've got a funny grandmother," Andy said, and he started up a side street. "Here's where I get off."

"I'll go with you," Joe said. "Hold it." And they darted up the side street together.

But there was no getting away from the crowds.

For this was Jerusalem, the most crowded city in the world.

Jerusalem was either crowded—

Or more crowded—

Or *most* crowded.

Depending on the time of the year, and what was going on.

And right now the most exciting week in all the year was here—the Feast of the Passover!

All the Jews all over the country came back to Jerusalem during that week to worship at the Temple. Even the Roman governor came fron Caesarea and moved into the castle for the week, to keep order.

Pontius Pilate himself!

And so they had been streaming in through the gate for days. People of every age and size and description:

Peasants from the surrounding villages,

Farmers and plowmen,

Rich owners of flocks and herds,

Merchants,

Tax collectors,

Ordinary people, extraordinary people, super-extraordinary people.

And beards of every description:

Pointed beards,

Spade-shaped beards,

Long, straggly beards,

Beards trimmed neat and close,

Beards trimmed every which way.

And faces of every description, too:

Indoor faces,

Outdoor faces,

Sand-blasted faces,

Happy faces,

3

Rich faces, poor faces, fat faces, thin faces.

No doubt about it. Jerusalem was *most* crowded. The ordinary crowds were swelled to bursting with pilgrims coming, some of them for the first time in their lives, to celebrate the Passover. All the inns were booked solid. Jerusalem was sort of wall-to-wall people, you might say, with standing room only. Joe and Andy were only a very small part of it. Like two little specks in the universe.

Joe was an orphan and his whole name was Joseph-Simon-Bar-Jason. Which meant he was named Joseph after one uncle and Simon after another uncle and Bar meant he was the son of his father Jason—

It was really quite complicated. A name like that could make you stoop-shouldered carrying it around. It was much quicker to call him Joe. He lived in Jerusalem with his grandmother in a small house snuggled against the city wall on the other side of town. The houses were all clustered together there as if they were frightened. And some of them were built right into the wall as if they had run in there to hide.

Andy's whole name was Andrew, with a string of names hitched on like you wouldn't believe.

Andy suited him much better.

The two boys hurried through the narrow shop-lined streets, up steps and down steps, through the stripes of sunshine and shadow. They listened to the grown-ups buying things at the sidewalk shops, shouting hysterically[2] over the purchase of a handful of dates as if they were buying Solomon's Temple itself.

"Big deal," said Andrew.

"You bet it is," said Joe. "Especially when you don't have much money. My grandmother buys things like that."

"So does my mother. She can haggle over buying something better than anybody I know."

"Not better than my grandmother. Around the house she's like a butterfly, soft and quiet. But when she's haggling over a bargain, she's a tiger."

2. They lost their cool.

4

They both laughed, imagining Grandmother, who weighed ninety-five pounds soaking wet, being a tiger.

"Is she really mad?" said Andy.

"Only dogs go mad."

"Well, then, is she really angry?"

"Noooo. She says it's all part of the fun. It makes her whole day."

They both laughed again. It was spring, there was excitement in the very air, and these were days when you burst out laughing over nothing at all. The winter rains were nearly over and the air wasn't too hot yet. Everybody was full of ginger, in a holiday mood. Even the sad-eyed little donkeys looked almost happy.

They came to a stop now. The great Temple loomed ahead, and the crowds were so dense that the traffic was at a standstill.

"Where'd they all come from?" Andy wanted to know. "They're here early. It's still six days till Passover."

"Lots of them come early to purify themselves and get ready," Joe said. "That's why all the inns are full. Why, it's—"

"Shhhhh."

"What's the matter?"

"SHHHHH."

Joe shushed. He raised his eyebrows at Andy. And Andy rolled his eyes toward the men just ahead and motioned to Joe to listen.

"Do you think that He will come?" one of them was saying.

"I can't believe He would dare," said another.

And another, "No, He wouldn't dare. Not right here in Jerusalem. He must know that He is a wanted man." Then they all began to talk at once.

"Why they put out a warrant for His arrest—how long ago?"

"A long time, now. Way back when He raised Lazarus from the dead."

"You mean when they *said* He raised Lazarus from the dead. We don't know that He really did it."

"Everyone says He did. I've talked with a lot of people who have seen Lazarus. Even though some people say he is in hiding."

"Anyhow the religious leaders put out a warrant. If anyone knows where Jesus of Nazareth is, please notify the chief priests and Pharisees at once."[3]

Joe froze in his tracks. They were talking about his Friend.

"They're talking about my Friend," he hissed to Andy.

"Jesus of Nazareth? The prophet?" Andy wanted to know.

"Yes. Jesus of Nazareth. Some say He is a prophet. And some say—"

"Some say?"

"Some say He's the Messiah. The Son of God. I've heard it. Many times. People whisper it."

"Well anyhow," Andy said. "They're laying for Him. If He decides to come here—"

"Well? What?"

"They'll arrest Him. That's what. That's what the man just said."

"He didn't say that," Joe's mouth was hanging open.

"Well that's what he meant," said Andy.

The crowd began to move again, and Joe and Andy were swept along with it. Along the street, then up the broad steps to the Temple, then into the huge Court of the Gentiles.

There, the confusion and noise was worse than in the streets. And there, Joe and Andy picked up the rest of the story. Bit by bit, they pieced it together.

Jesus of Nazareth was in Bethany, at that moment.

He and His disciples were having dinner that very night at the house of Simon.

Who Simon?

Why Simon, the leper, whom Jesus had healed.

Jesus' close friends, Mary and Martha, were serving the dinner.

And Jesus was an honored guest. And another honored guest was— Lazarus!

Jesus had raised him from the dead. *And there he was—living proof of Jesus' power!*

Tongues in the Temple court were wagging.

Would Jesus come to Jerusalem?

3. See John 11:57.

And what would happen if He did?

"Wow!" said Joe. Bethany was only two miles away. "Wow!"

"What do you think?" said Andy.

"I don't know what to think," said Joe. "Just wow."

So THAT'S why Grandmother's bones were twanging.

"Something's going to happen this week," she had said. "I just feel it in my bones."

When Grandmother's bones twanged, you'd better duck.

Something always happened.

# Chapter Two

# FRIDAY-
# LATER

Grandmother sat at the foot of Joe's bed, which was a mat stretched out on the floor in the corner of the room. The sun had gone down now, and the Sabbath had begun.[1]

Grandmother had her head bowed, but she was watching Joe. He was sitting on his bed, his knees drawn up. His elbows were on his knees and his fists were squinched into his cheeks. He was frowning in fierce concentration.

"Tell me about the Passover," he said. "The very first one."

He needn't have asked. Every Jewish boy heard the story of the first Passover, every year at Passover time. But he did anyhow. Grandmother liked to be asked; it was sort of a ritual.[2]

"All right," she said, and she cleared her throat (She always did—it was part of the ritual.), and began. "Once, a long, long time ago, our people were slaves in Egypt."

"Ohhhhh," he said. (That was part of the ritual too.)

---

1. The Sabbath began at sundown on Friday and lasted until sundown on Saturday.
2. It was a little routine they went through.

"And our leader Moses had gone to the Pharaoh many times to ask him to let them go free."

Joe nodded. He knew it by heart.

"Well. *One* day,"—ah, now, the story was beginning—"God had had just about enough. He'd given Pharaoh many chances to let our people go. Now Pharaoh was going to have to do it the hard way.

"Ah HAH," said Joe, and he stretched out flat, his hands under his head, to hear the rest.

"Moses *warned* Pharaoh," Grandmother reminded Joe, "He *told* him what would happen."

Joe nodded again. He remembered.

"But Pharaoh would not listen. Sooooo—"

Grandmother plunged into the rest of the story, her eyes bright, her hands going through all the motions. Every family had to get a lamb, God said. A *perfect* lamb, without blemish.[3] And kill it. And sprinkle the blood on the doorposts of their homes.

And that night they were to eat roast lamb,

And bitter herbs,

And bread *without yeast.*[4]

They were to eat with their traveling clothes on, prepared for a long journey,

Wearing walking shoes and carrying walking sticks, ready to GET GOING when the signal was given.

BECAUSE—

That very night, the angel of death would go through the land and take the oldest son in every family. EXCEPT in the homes where the blood was on the door. "When I see the blood," God had said, "I will *pass over you* and you will not be punished."

And sure enough.

That very night, the angel of death—

Grandmother always made that part so spooky that Joe's eyeballs bulged out and his fingertips tingled.

Phew!

3. Without anything wrong with it.
4. No time for yeast; the bread would take too long to rise!

10

The angel of death passed through Egypt. And the cries could be heard throughout the land.

BUT.

Not one Israelite home was touched.

Their safety had all hinged on the lamb.

The lamb that was killed, and the blood that was sprinkled on the door.

"You must celebrate this Passover feast every year," God had said. "For it will cause you always to remember when I brought you out of the land of Egypt. And tell your children, so *they'll* remember."

Yes, indeed.

"And so we celebrate it every year," Grandmother said. "The Feast of the Passover is the most important—*the* most important Feast of all."

The story was over.

"And now, to sleep with you, Joseph. Tomorrow we must be early at the Temple. It is the Sabbath. The most important day in all the week."

She leaned down, and Joe kissed her on both cheeks. Her skin was soft, soft, like old wrinkled leather. But her eyes sparkled young.

She went out the door, and Joe could hear her outside, talking softly with the neighbor women.

He thought about the lamb again. Every morning a lamb was slain on the altar at the Temple. And on the Sabbath, two lambs were slain. God, thought Joe as he began to drift off, was certainly interested in lambs.

Tomorrow was the Sabbath day.

A quiet day.

Grandmother had done all her baking and cooking today because on the Sabbath she could not light a fire.

The things you couldn't do on the Sabbath.

Phew!

You couldn't sew two stitches (and who could get anything done with *one* stitch?).

11

You couldn't tie a knot  unless it was a knot that could be untied with one hand.

You couldn't write two letters.

Or sock anything with a hammer.

Or carry anything from one property to another.

Or catch a deer.

Or sow seed.

Or plow.

Or thresh grain, or grind it, or sift it.

Or shear wool or wash it or beat it.

Or spin it.

You couldn't even *spit*.

Not because spitting wasn't polite.[5]

But because you might make a dent in the ground, and that would be plowing.

Joe thought of all these things you could not do, and more, as he was drifting off. God had not said you couldn't do those things. The Pharisees had made up all those crazy laws. God had merely said to keep the Sabbath holy.

Some laws, Joe thought.

Even the rabbis had thought of ways to get around them. You couldn't travel more than two miles? Easy. They just put some food at the two-mile mark *before* the Sabbath. Then they declared that spot a temporary dwelling place. So they could go right past without breaking the law.

His friend Jesus of Nazareth wasn't like that at all.

Joe wondered if Jesus and His disciples and Lazarus and Martha and Mary had had a good time at that dinner party. And he wondered too about the gossip. Would Jesus dare to come to Jerusalem?

And what if He did?

Would they arrest Him?

Grandmother and the women's voices continued softly, outside the window.

Joe was asleep.

5. Which of course it wasn't.

12

# Chapter Three

# SATURDAY

Early morning was best in Jerusalem.

Even before daybreak, the people were shuffling quietly through the streets, toward the Temple area. Inside the Temple—*way* inside, in the holy place—a priest would burn incense on the golden altar. Outside, the people would gather quietly to pray.

The ceremony was always the same.

The captain of the Temple would ask one of the priests to go up to one of the high points in the Temple and look out over the east to see if the sun had risen yet.

Then everyone would wait. Finally—

"The morning shines already!" the priest would call back.

"Does it light up the sky as far as Hebron?" the captain would ask.

"Yea—as far as Hebron!"

That was the signal.

The orders flew thick and fast.

"Bring in the lamb to be slain!"

13

"Open the gates of the Temple!"

And everything seemed to happen at once.

The lamb was brought in.

The Temple gates were unlocked and thrown open.

The silver trumpets began to blast, splitting the sky and sending late sleepers all over Jerusalem tumbling from their mats.

The priests poured into the Temple, each one to his duties—polishing candlesticks, cleaning the altar of incense—

And the lamb was slain.

Then the Ten Commandments were recited, solemn and frightening, and the rest of the sacrifices were started—the meal offering and the oil and the wine.

And then—

MUSIC!

You never heard such music as they had those days in Jerusalem!

First the silver trumpets were sounded, and then it all began.

Flutes,

Cymbals,

Ram's horns,

Lyres,

Harps,

Oboes.

AND CHOIRS!

You can't imagine how great they were. Magnificent![1]

Every singer was handpicked, and had to have five years of training before he was allowed to sing as much as a "mi-mi-mi-mi" in public. They would divide in groups and sing the psalms back and forth to each other, until they split the heavens.

> "It is a good thing
>    To give thanks unto the Lord. . . ."[2]

Oh, yes, early morning was best in Jerusalem.

1 Super!
2. See Psalm 92.

Even before daybreak.
There was no doubt about it.

_____

Joe stirred on his mat in the corner when he heard it. The rays
from the rising sun had sneaked in through the windows of Grandmother's house. The air was cool and moist from the night. Grandmother was nowhere about.

The lamb was being slain. Only this was the Sabbath. It would
be two lambs this morning.

Joe scrambled to his feet, and poured water from a pitcher, to
wash.

God, he thought as he splashed and gurgled, was certainly interested in lambs.

# Chapter 4

# SUNDAY

Joe was walking backwards so he could see where he'd been.

Which didn't matter, for at that moment he didn't know whether he was coming or going anyhow.

What a day!

It was the first day of the week. One day closer to the day of the Feast of the Passover. And the crowds were streaming into the city from all directions, more than ever.

The whole area was one big traffic jam, bumper to bumper. Donkeys, people, camels, people, carriages, people, caravans, people—

The sidewalk shops were spilling their wares out of their doorways—

Rugs,

Bread,

Olives,

Guts,

Dates,

Silks,

Grape leaves,

Camels' feet,

Milk,

Spices,

Grapes,

And sheep and lambs all over the place.

17

The sun had been up for hours. The singing of the morning psalm from the Temple had started his day. "The earth is the Lord's"[1] had come billowing over the air like giant waves. He had washed and splashed and gurgled and done his chores and eaten his breakfast, and now he was out to jostle with the crowds and smell the smells and catch the gossip—

But never in his wildest dreams had he expected to catch gossip like *this*.

He had gotten it in bits and snitches, and everyone was too big or too old or in too much of a hurry to ask.

Then he saw Andy.

He fought his way around two donkeys, some women juggling huge goatskin bags of milk, and a man with a cartload of bread as high as a small palm tree.

"Andy!"

"Joe ole boy! I've been looking for you!"

They pumped all four hands as if they had not seen each other for a week.

"Guess who's coming!" Andy said.

"I know, I know! Jesus the prophet! Jesus my friend!" Joe pumped some more. And then he sobered. "Do you think they'll arrest Him?"

"No!" Andy laughed. "Everyone is talking about how wonderful He is! He has more followers than ever before. They're all coming with Him, and the crowd gets bigger by the minute. I heard as much."

"Where are they now?" Joe wanted to know. "Are they here?"

"They're almost here." Andy pulled Joe out of the traffic and they edged their way along the wall toward the nearest city gate. Now they were carried along by the crowd; everyone seemed to be going their way.

"Where's everybody going?" Joe said.

"Out to meet Him! Come *on!*"

Why not?

Why not indeed!

1. See Psalm 24.

Out the gate they went, and up the road with the crowd toward the Mount of Olives. And they huffed and they puffed—and they listened.

And watched.

"There He comes! See—way up there!"

"He's riding on a donkey!"

Joe and Andy fell over a branch, leaped to their feet.

"They're spreading their robes along the way for Him!"

"They've spread some robes on the donkey for His saddle!"

"A donkey! A donkey! A king would ride in on a donkey!"

Joe and Andy fell over each other, scrambled to their feet.

"That's it! A king! God has given us a king!"

"Of course! The prophets said, 'For look—your King is coming. He is the Righteous One, the Victor! Yet he is lowly, riding on a donkey's colt!²' The prophets said it—and now here He is!"

Joe and Andy tripped on their own sandals, staggered to their feet.

"I'm down more than I'm up," said Andy.

"Did the prophets say that?" Joe wanted to know.

"I think so," said Andy, wiping the sweat off his face with his sleeve.

"But wouldn't a king ride in on a horse? King David would have ridden in on a horse, I'll bet," said Joe.

"A warrior king would ride in on a horse. He's a peaceful king, I guess." Andy always seemed to know everything.

"How do you know?" said Joe.

"I listen," said Andy.

And they both tripped over a rock and went splat.

Phew.

People were waving things now. Palm branches! People had torn branches from the trees on the way. Joe and Andy scrambled for some that had dropped to the ground.

"Long live the King!" the people were shouting.

"Let all heaven rejoice! Glory to God in the highest heavens!"

2. See Zechariah 9:9.

Andy got to his feet first. "Glory to God in the highest!" he shouted, waving his branch. "God bless the King of Israel!" He looked down at Joe. "Get with it," he said. "Put your sandal on."

"I can't," said Joe. "You're standing on it."

---

Later, as they got to Jerusalem, the shouting had turned to chanting and singing. It rose in one great chorus that shook the heavens. Joe had recovered his sandal and the two boys were waving their palm branches now, and singing, too, picking up the words in snitches, their faces red and damp, their hearts throbbing. This was no ordinary parade, no ordinary excitement. There was something about it that made Joe's blood leap in his veins. He never knew he could sing before; his voice had wings.

Through the Golden Gate they went, the crowd and Joe and Andy—packed together and straining against the sides of the opening as if they would burst it apart to get through.

A king?

A king! Yes, a king! To save them and set up His kingdom and rescue them from the hated Roman rulers. It was here! It was here at last—the deliverance that the prophets had promised! Before their very eyes, it was happening!

And so Jesus of Nazareth entered Jerusalem, through the Golden Gate and into the Temple area. Joe and Andy were shucked off the edge of the crowd like the husks off an ear of corn. They waved their branches mightily and they jumped up and down to get glimpses over the crowd and they would have climbed up people's backs if they could. But they were only boys, after all. Though sometimes they *felt* six feet tall, it just wasn't so. And so at last they gave up and dropped behind, their palm branches drooping at their sides.

"Did you see Him?" said Andy.

"No." Joe stooped to fix the sandal that wouldn't stay on. "Only the top of His head. I didn't see Him at all."

They parted then, for it was getting late in the afternoon; they'd been away from home long enough. Joe walked a few feet, switching his palm branch against the building. Then he turned.

21

"But I *felt* Him " he yelled. And then he headed for Grandmother's house.

"I really didn't touch Him," he thought as he walked along. "I just *felt* Him. I felt as if He was looking at me, even though He didn't turn His head." The thought filled him with a strange excitement. He fought his way up the street; he was bucking the crowd now. It was a long time before they thinned out and he could amble. Joe liked to amble, zigzagging and taking his time and breathing in all the smells—the garlic and the roasting meat and the spices and the sweat. And he liked to nose around in the sidewalk shops. They weren't crowded now; everyone who could move had gone toward the Temple to see what all the hullabaloo was about.

Boy, what a day. *What a day!* There hadn't been anything like it since he could remember. When Pontius Pilate had moved in from Caesarea, it hadn't caused such a stir as that. This day had been exciting from the moment he'd opened his eyes this morning, right up to the moment he'd seen Jesus of Nazareth go through that gate—

Joe stopped in his tracks.

And thought of the music that had been sung this morning at the morning sacrifice.

"Open up, O ancient gates, and let the King of Glory in.
Who is this King of Glory?
The Lord, strong and mighty . . .
Yes, open wide the gates and let the King of Glory in."[3]

That was always sung on the first day of the week. But this morning it seemed special, somehow.

Then Joe saw it. The chicken.

There was a crate of them on the sidewalk—baby chicks, and they were turning in circles and pushing each other, all trying to get out, their little heads poking out between the slats.

But the thing that made this chick different was that he was outside

3. See Psalm 24.

22

trying to get *in*. Somehow he'd gotten out, and he was frantic, trying to get back where he came from.

"What's the matter, fella?" Joe said, squatting, his hands stretched out. "What's the matter? Run away and change your mind?" He tried to close in, but the chick was zigging and zagging. "Come on, you little rascal. Heeeeeey." The chick flapped his budding wings and took frantic leaps in every direction. And then—

"Gotcha."

Joe straightened up, the little ball of yellow feathers warm in his cupped hands.

"Awwwww. Come on. I won't hurt you."

He stroked his little head until its frantic "peeps" quieted down, then stopped.

And right then and there, Joe wanted a baby chick more than he wanted anything else in the world.

He looked up the street. Down. Across. Up and down again.

And then he tucked the chick in his tunic. It felt soft and warm against his belly. And he sauntered a few steps away from the shop. And then he quickened his pace a little, until he was safely around the corner. His heart was beating fast. No one had seen him.

---

"Joseph Simon Bar-Jason!" It was Grandmother's voice, from inside the house.

Joe stopped short. There'd be no time to hide the chick.

"Aren't you a little late? I've been waiting for you."

Oh, good grief. She was coming out.

"I have a lot to tell you!" he called. But she was in the doorway now, drying her hands on the towel draped around her waist.

"I have a lot to tell *you*," she said, her eyes merry. "I've a surprise for you. It's in the—what's the matter?"

Joe had begun to itch. The chick was walking around.

"Nothing, Grandmother."

"Well, then. Come around back. I've brought you—Joseph Simon, there IS something!"

"No, Grand—" (Oh, good grief. The chick was peeping)—"no,

23

Grandmother." He folded his arms across his chest, trying to keep the chick in one place.

"No (another peep) Grandmother," he finished weakly.

She looked at him, her head cocked to one side.

"What do you have in your blouse?"

"I don't have any—" (peep) "—I don't have—" (another peep. Crazy chick!)

"A baby chick. I have a baby chick," Joe began to fish in his tunic. The chick thrashed wildly until his hand closed around it. He pulled it out and made a cradle for it in his cupped hands.

"What a fuzzy little fellow," Grandmother said. "Did somebody give it to you?"

Joe swallowed carefully.

"Well, you see," he began, "there I was, walking home and minding my business, when—you're not going to believe this, but along came—"

The singing from the Temple came floating through the air. It was too far away to be heard plainly. But they knew every word by heart.

*"Open up, O ancient gates, and let the King of Glory in—"*

"Along came a lady with these chicks—"

*"Who is this King of Glory . . . the Lord strong and mighty . . ."*

"And she asked me—she asked me—"

*"Yes, open wide the gates and let the King of Glory in."*

Now they would burn the incense. They always burned the incense last during the evening sacrifice. The lamb had already been slain.

The last note died away.

Joe looked up at Grandmother. The chick stirred in his hands.

"I stole it," he said simply.

# Chapter Five

# SUNDAY–MONDAY

Joe and his grandmother stood staring at each other for a moment.
And then at the chick.

And then back at each other.

Her eyes had more surprise in them than anger. It was as if she simply couldn't believe he had done it. He had done it all right, and the chick peeped again as if to prove it.

"Put the little fellow down," said Grandmother. "In here will do." She pointed to a clay pot. Joe put the chick in it, and it immediately began to climb frantically up the rounded sides and slide back down again.

Now those were the days when grown-ups were grown-ups and frustrations[1] hadn't been invented yet and they weren't afraid of fracturing your future or giving you inflammation of the phobia. When you did something wrong—zap—you were punished right then and there.

---

1. Ask your Mother. No, ask your Father when your Mother's not around.

"Go get the switch," she said.

Joe went, dragging his feet. "Such a little thing," he muttered. "Just a baby chick. You could hold it in one hand."

"Stealing is stealing," she said. "*What* you steal is quite beside the point."

He came back with the switch and handed it to her. "If you refuse to discipline your son, it proves you don't love him—" she started. And Joe chimed in.[2] "—for if you love him you will be prompt to punish him." They both finished together. "It's in the Scriptures," she reminded him.

She went into the house and Joe followed.

Rats.

Why had he ever seen the chick in the first place? Why hadn't he gone up another street?

He was glad when it was over.

One thing about Grandmother, you had to admit, she didn't stay angry very long. "There, now," she said. "I'm sorry I had to do that, Joe. But taking something that doesn't belong to you is stealing. And stealing is sin. And sin must be punished."

"I know, I know," said Joe, staring at the ground.

"Well. Now. Come see the surprise I have for you. I was just about to bring her in the house for the night. She's out here in this box."

"Something for me?" Joe scrambled out after her, his humiliation forgotten. Grandmother outscrambled him, though, and got there first. "She's in this box," she said proudly. And sure enough, she was.

"A real big live chicken. A real grown-up one!" Joe's mouth was gaping open. "Is he a boy chicken or a girl chicken?"

"Well, I hope she's a girl chicken," Grandmother said. "She's sitting on eggs."

And then Joe saw her outspread wings. "Eggs? Eggs with chickens in them? How many are there? And where did you get him?"

---

2. Well he didn't exactly "chime" in. He sort of "muttered" in. He didn't feel like chiming.

"Uncle Simon. But I'll tell you about that later. Twenty eggs. And they're due to hatch in a few days. And when they do hatch, you'll have—"

"Twenty baby chicks! Yes?"

"Twenty baby chicks—no. Sixteen baby chicks, yes."

"What d'you mean, sixteen baby chicks?"

"The law of Moses says 'four for one.' That means if you steal something, you give back four times as much as you stole. And besides that, you tell the person you stole from that you're sorry. Get it?"

"Oh, boy. I'm going to call him Molly."

"It's a her."

"May I build a coop for him?"

"It's a her, Joe."

"Twenty baby chicks."

"Did you hear what I've been telling you?"

"Sixteen baby chicks. May I start building a coop for him first thing in the morning?"

"It's a her."

"I can't identify with girls."

"Well anyhow, not the first thing. We have other matters to attend to."

"What other matters?"

"Well first you must return the chick you stole to the shopkeeper."

"Yes, Grandmother."

"And you must tell him that you're sorry."

"Yes."

"And you must tell him that as soon as your chicks are hatched you'll give him four to make up for the one you took."

"Yes. I was listening. To all that you said."

"And then we're going down to the Temple. I have some things to explain to you."

"Yes, Grandmother," he said. But he was thinking. "Sixteen baby chicks. Oh, boy." He'd never owned anything like that in his life before. Sixteen, WOW, sixteen baby chicks. And Molly ole boy was going to hatch them.

He scrambled about doing his evening chores and whistling. He made a bed of soft grass right in the clay pot for the baby chick and brought it in for the night. He fed both the baby chick and Molly ole boy some grain. He clucked happily over both of them. He lighted the lamp and brought in some water and chattered like a magpie as he and Grandmother sat down to the evening meal.

"Did you hear about what went on in town today?" he said to Grandmother.

"Hear about it? I went down to see it. I heard the gossip, but I didn't see much of anything. The crowds were too great. I just stood on the edge. Did you see, Joseph?"

"See? I went outside the gates and up the road to meet Him. It was my friend, Jesus of Nazareth. The prophet. They were hailing Him as a king!"

"Ohhhhh, mercy," said Grandmother. "That's impossible."

"But they were! They were shouting 'Blessed is He who comes in the name of the Lord.' And they were chanting 'Save us.' They were *chanting* it. Like this: 'Save us, save us, save us—'"

"Joe. Eat your food."

"Well they were," he went on, munching happily. "Some even say He is the promised Messiah. And He's coming to set up His kingdom right here—"

"Joe!"

"—and right now—"

*"Joseph!"*

"Well that's what they're saying," Joe insisted. "And if He does, He'll get us out from under the Roman rule and—"

Grandmother turned away to scrape the last of the stew from the pot. "You're talking nonsense, Joseph," she said. She always called him Joseph when she was upset.

"Then He went on into the Temple," said Joe, "and I couldn't see any more. It was getting late and I had to come home. But I almost saw Him. I saw the back of His head. He was riding on a donkey. Just like a king."

"Tomorrow," Grandmother said, "we'll go to the Temple. First thing in the morning." As if the subject were closed.

Joe said no more about it. He washed, got into his night clothes and got ready for bed. He knelt at his mat, Grandmother standing over him. And prayed the prayer every Jewish boy learned from his mother's knee.

"Father, into Your hands I commend my spirit," he said solemnly.

———————————————

The next morning, on the way to the Temple, Joe and Grandmother picked up the gossip. The awful ordeal[3] of returning the baby chick to the shopowner had to be done on the way. Joe promised that he'd bring four chicks more as soon as "Molly ole boy" hatched them. Grandmother stood behind Joe, her hands folded in front of her, and nodded, but she didn't say a word. Joe had to do the whole dreadful thing all by himself.

Phew.

The gossip was that Jesus of Nazareth had left the Temple the night before and had gone back to Bethany with His disciples to stay with His friends—Martha and Mary and their brother Lazarus.

As Joe and Grandmother neared the Temple area, the crowds were so great, they held hands tightly so they could keep together. Up the steps and into the jam-packed Court of the Gentiles. Phew! The Court of the Gentiles was always noisy, but it was worse than ever before. Goats and pigeons and doves and lambs—shut up in crates and tied up with ropes. And people! From every nation in the world and from all the outside provinces[4]—and each one jabbering in his own language and his own dialect. It all added up to one big mishmash—and the result was total confusion.

And such business going on!

Each family that came had to buy an animal for sacrifice. And the outer courts of the Temple area were where they had to buy them.

And who did the selling?

The priests and the religious leaders of the Temple.

———

3. Something you just hate to do.
4. Like states.

And who got all the profits?

You guessed it. The priests and the religious leaders of the Temple.

So the Temple courts were jammed with stalls, and the prices were outrageous.[5]

But that wasn't the worst of it.

People who came from far away had another money problem. Their money was not like the money in Jerusalem. So the court was also cluttered with the tables of the moneychangers. And did the moneychangers cheat? You'd better believe they did. They exchanged foreign money for shekels all right; the problem was that at the end of the deal the people always found themselves a few shekels short.[6] It was like trying to change a dollar and getting only sixty cents back.

Now all of this could have been done outside the Temple courts. There was a perfectly good bazaar outside, and plenty of space. But they had long ago moved into the courts as a matter of convenience. And the whole thing had grown into one gigantic racket.

Scandalous!

Joe and Grandmother threaded their way through this crowd. Joe acted as a buffer and hung fast to her hand so she could follow him through the opening. They finally made their way up to the next court, which was the Court of the Women. It was rough going now. They could hardly keep on their feet. The people jostled past carrying their animals for sacrifices to the priests.

They made their way slowly across, and then finally to the edge of the Court of Israel where the great brazen altar was. The priests were doing a brisk business too. Or it looked to Joe more like a business than an act of worship. Into that court they could not go, but they could climb some steps and look over the wall. People were straining forward, carrying their doves or their lambs, whatever they could afford. Joe watched as a man held up the lamb he was carrying, put his hand on it solemnly, and then handed it to the Temple priest.

5. They were sky-high and you'd better believe it.
6. Try saying "a few shekels short" fast five times.

30

"WHAT'S HE DOING?" Joe asked.

"Shhhhhh!"

"What's he doing?"

"He's transferring his sin to the lamb," said Grandmother.

"What for?"

"The lamb will be killed in his place. It's God's Law. Sin must be punished." They looked at each other for a moment, thinking of the stolen chick. "There is no forgiveness of sin without the shedding of blood," she said. "You see what I mean?"

Yes, Joe got the idea. He was solemn and quiet as they turned and made their way through the Court of the Women, back down the steps to the Court of the Gentiles.

Then they stopped in their tracks.

What was going on?

The animals were stampeding, scattering in all directions, their owners scurrying after them. Everyone was making for the nearest gate to get out of there as fast as possible.

Then there was the crash of wood and the jingle of coins. Someone was kicking over the tables of the moneychangers!

Crash!

The tables went sprawling, one after another!

Whop!

The stalls where the doves were being sold went tumbling over!

Woosh!

People and money and doves and sheep and lambs and crates went tumbling pell-mell across the huge court, like leaves before a hurricane! And people who were coming in with loads of merchandise, stopped in their tracks and backed their carts up, their eyes goggling.

What was causing it all?

And then they saw.

It wasn't *what*. It was *who*.

It was a man—His back was to them. And He was brandishing[7] a whip made out of ropes. And He was shouting. And His shouts

7. Waving.

were punctuated with swift kicks at the moneychangers' tables and stalls. "It is written in the Scriptures," He shouted, "My Temple is to be a place of prayer for all nations—"

Bash went another table.

"—but you have turned it into a *den of robbers!*"

Who could argue with that? It *did* say that in the Scriptures. Nobody dared answer Him. Joe and Grandmother and the people all around them were struck dumb for a moment. Then some of them found their tongues.

"Who is He?"

"It's Jesus of Nazareth!"

Joe's ears went up to points, and he listened harder.

"He's back from Bethany."

"Did you hear—some are calling Him a king!"

"He acts like a king! Where does He get the authority?"

That's what the leaders of the Temple wanted to know, too. They ground their teeth in rage.

"I wonder why they don't arrest Him?" Grandmother thought. "It would be the easiest thing in the world."

Grandmother didn't know it, but that would have been the hardest thing in the world. Too many people were excited about Him. Too many people thought He was the Messiah. Arrest Him now, and they might have a riot on their hands. They just didn't dare.

Joe and Grandmother thought they would never get through the tangle of people, animals and upturned tables and stalls, but finally they did. The hubbub was just as bad outside. People who were coming to see what the commotion[8] was all about got mixed up with the people who were trying to get away from it. The result was a wild whirlwind of people.

It was a struggle against wall-to-wall people almost all the way home. "I thought sure they were going to arrest Him," she said again to no one in particular.

They walked along in silence past the shops. "But I'm awfully glad they didn't," she said finally.

8. Big rumpus.

"You're glad they didn't?" Joe asked.

"Well," she said, "the Temple *is* God's house. And it *is* a place of prayer. And buying those doves and lambs to take to the altar is a form of worship. It's an *act* of worship. And—and—it *has* become a racket—a shameful racket. It's just as well somebody came along and put a stop to it. And if this Jesus was the one to do it, well—" She sputtered and then stopped. They walked in silence for a few seconds. And then—

"Grandmother," Joe said. "I think you *enjoyed* it. I think you enjoyed the whole thing."

"Wellllll—when you're fighting for the right—sometimes I enjoy a good scrap," she said.

"Grandmother!" Joe giggled. "You ought to be spanked."

Grandmother didn't answer. But her eyes were merry.

# Chapter Six

# TUESDAY

That afternoon Joe and Andy built a coop for Molly ole boy.

They took some short slats and some long slats.

They sawed the long slats the length they thought they ought to be.

Measure? Who had time to measure.

So now the long slats became the short slats and the short slats became the long slats.

So they sawed the short slats which were now the long slats to the length they thought they ought to be.

So now the long slats became the short slats again. And the short slats became the long slats.

By the time they were finished they had made the most lopsided, crooked, out-of-shape, askew, wonderful chicken coop you ever saw. They had only one problem. Each time the long slats had become the short slats, the coop got smaller. So Molly ole boy didn't have much room to turn around.

They put some straw on the bottom and coaxed her off her nest. Then, very carefully, they began to move the eggs. "Don't turn them, don't turn them," said Grandmother, who had come running out of the house to watch.

"Why not?"

"Because she turns them herself. And she knows exactly how to do it, and when."

"How does she know?" said Andy.

"Well God tells her," said Grandmother, "She was just born knowing how to do these things."

"Hatched," said Joe.

"Hatched, then," said Grandmother.

So, without turning the eggs, they put them carefully on the straw. And coaxed Molly ole boy into her new house. They squatted down to see her. "The slats are kind of crooked," said Andy.

"Well when you're squatted down you can see how crooked they are," said Joe. "But when you're standing up they don't look so bad."

Grandmother chuckled behind them. "Everything looks fine from up here," she said.

"How's everything, Molly ole boy?" Joe called in. "D'you like it?"

"Awwwww-puk-puk," said Molly ole boy. "I can put up with it. Things are rough all over."

"Well, think about hatching those chickens," said Joe. "We're expecting them this week." Was he imagining things or did Molly ole boy snort? She had a wicked look of mischief in her eyes. She was going to be a hard one to handle, no doubt about it.

Joe and Andy straightened up. "Any errands, Grandmother?" Joe said.

"Noooo," Grandmother said. "The afternoon's nearly gone. You're off the hook for the rest of the day."

Joe and Andy were half a block down the street before she could change her mind.

"I was looking for you yesterday," Andy said. "But the crowd was so big it was like looking for a needle in a haystack. There was almost a riot down in the Temple court. That's where I was. That's where I was looking for you."

"I was there too," said Joe. "With Grandmother. Watching the sacrifices. She explained all over again how you transferred your sin to the lamb. That the lamb was killed in your place. I knew it already. It's one of those things you have to be told again. You forget."

"I know," Andy said. "I usually get told right after I've done something wrong."

They walked along in silence for a minute. Then, "What did you do, Joe?"

This was humiliating.[1]

"I stole a baby chick," Joe said, and he told about it. Only he made it sound as if the chick had jumped right up into his hand as he was walking past the shop minding his own business.

"What did your Grandmother do, Joe?"

"She took me to the Temple."

"I mean besides that?"

Oh, rats.

"You remember King David prayed, 'Purge me with hyssop' "?

"Yeah."

"Well Grandmother purged me with an olive switch."

"What?"

"She clobbered me. I was just trying to be funny. And there's nothing funny about it. I mean I really feel bad about it. I shouldn't have done it."

Silence. Then,

"She packs quite a wallop," Joe said thoughtfully. "But you don't mind too much. Because you know she loves you."

"Does she always use the olive switch?" Andy wanted to know.

"No," said Joe. "She hardly ever uses it. She punishes me in other ways."

"Except when you steal something," said Andy.

"Yes. She didn't go for that at all."

"Jesus of Nazareth wasn't very gentle yesterday," said Andy. "Did you hear what He did?"

---

1. It embarrassed Joe to have to admit it.

"I saw what He did," Joe said. "He kicked all the moneychangers' tables over."

"And broke up the stalls," Andy added.

By this time they had reached the entrance to the Court of the Gentiles. They went in on tiptoe, as if they expected something dreadful to happen. The court was crowded, but the volume on the noise had been turned down considerably.

"It's pretty tidy here," said Joe. "I think we're in the wrong place."

"You know," said Andy, "I think everybody's afraid of Him."

"Noooo, Andy. They're not afraid of Him. The people love Him. They're all with Him 100 percent. It's the Temple priests and the religious leaders who are afraid of Him. They're afraid because the people think He's a king."

"Well He sounds like a king," said Andy. "And He acts like a king. Maybe He *is* a king."

"Maybe He's the Messiah," said Joe. "Maybe He's—"

He stopped and grabbed Andy's arm. "Look!" he said.

"Where?"

"Over there. Solomon's porch. It's Jesus of Nazareth Himself. He's back from Bethany again."

By this time they were on the edge of the crowd around Jesus, and they began to worm their way in.

Jesus was talking, and the people were hanging on His every word. All kinds of people. Well-dressed, many of them. But there were poor people and crippled people and blind people and beggars, too.

Oh, good grief.

Some very important people were in a tight little group by themselves, way up front. And they looked as if they had just lunched on a can of worms and chased them down with vinegar. The priests and religious leaders of the Temple!

Auuuuugh.

"Listen to this story," Jesus was saying.[2]

---

2. The stories that Jesus told are called parables. A parable is a short story that teaches a truth.

The people shushed each other and edged closer.

"Once there was a landowner," Jesus said. "And he planted a vineyard with the choicest of vines, so that when they grew and bore fruit, the grapes would be the choicest of grapes. He put a hedge around it so nobody could get in. And he built a tall platform for a watchman to climb up and watch for wild animals and robbers."

The people listened, nodding. They knew all about vineyards.

"And he rented the vineyard to some farmers," Jesus went on. "And then he went to live in another country."

Joe picked up his ears. His uncle Simon rented a vineyard exactly like that, outside Jerusalem, up in the hills. And he rented it from a wealthy landowner who lived in another country! *Exactly* like that. And when the grape harvest came, Uncle Simon hired men to pick the grapes. And instead of paying rent with money, Uncle Simon paid it with part of the grape harvest. The wealthy landowner sent his servants to collect his share of the grapes, every harvest time. And Uncle Simon had a watchtower too. And he hired watchmen to watch at night so thieves wouldn't get in. Sometimes he watched up there himself.

"Well, the grape harvest came," Jesus was saying, "and the wealthy landowner sent his servants to the farmer to collect his share of the crop. And do you know what happened?"

"No," Joe cried out, "what happened?" before he thought. Everyone went "SHHHHH!" and heads were turned to stare at him and he felt about as big as a mite.[3]

"But the farmers attacked his servants," Jesus said, "and they beat them, and stoned them. One of them was even killed."

They waited to hear the rest. It was very quiet.

"Then the landowner sent a larger group of his servants to collect the grapes."

Their eyes were big, waiting.

"And the same thing happened all over again. The servants were beaten and stoned and killed. And then—"

Everybody waited.

---

3. A mite was the least valuable coin in Palestine. Like our penny.

"And then," Jesus went on, "the landowner sent his own son. 'Surely,' he said, 'if I send my own son, they'll respect *him*. They'll accept *him.*' And what happened?"

"What happened?" Joe whispered. He didn't dare say it aloud this time.

"When these farmers saw the son coming," Jesus' voice was sad now, "they said among themselves, 'This vineyard will belong to *him* some day. Let's kill him. Yes—let's kill him and get it for ourselves.' So they dragged him out of the vineyard. And killed him."

The people were still listening, open-mouthed. But now Jesus turned to the religious leaders. "When he returns, what do you think he'll do to those farmers? What do you think they deserve?"

A great silence, a long silence this time.

The religious leaders stared at the ground, then down into their hearts. They did not look at each other; they did not dare look at Him. And not one of them dared to answer His question.

Finally,

"He will kill the renters," Jesus said, "and rent the land to others."

The religious leaders stiffened. How *dare* He tell a story like that? How dare He point to them—

For He *was* pointing to them. *They* were the wicked farmers in His story, and they jolly well knew it. Their fists itched and their beards prickled with the desire to arrest Him, right then and there. But they didn't dare. For they knew today what they'd known yesterday. If they arrested Him, they'd have a riot on their hands. So they pulled their robes about them and straightened up and stalked off like a string of angry camels.[4]

"Andy," said Joe, "the landowner is God."

"The landowner is *who?*"

"The landowner is God. And we're the vines."

Every little Jewish boy knew that Israel was called a vineyard. They'd been taught that from the moment they could understand. They sang it in the synagogues:

4. Did you ever look a camel in the face? He looks as if he'd like to spit on you. And if you get too close—he will!

41

"You brought us from Egypt
As though we were a tender vine . . .
You cleared the ground and tilled the soil,
And we took root and filled the land . . ."[5]


"But who are the farmers?" Andy whispered back.

Joe couldn't answer. "Whoever they are," he said, "they're up to no good. They killed the landowner's servants and—oh, oh."

"What?" said Andy.

"Who are the servants? I don't know that either."

"Could we ask Him?"

"We couldn't even get near Him. Besides it's getting late. We'd better head for home."

On the way home they hurried, for it was later than they realized. The afternoon was gone.

"Phew," said Andy as they hurried along. "The farmers took care of the vines. They were responsible for the vines. But who they were I don't know—you're not listening, Joe."

"This is the shop where I stole that crazy chick. I wish he hadn't run out in front of me like that. If I had it to do over again I'd just hurry past or try to poke him back in the crate."

"You'd probably break his neck," said Andy.

"That's probably one of the things those farmers did to the landowner's servants," said Joe, getting back to the story. "Grandmother could figure it out. Who everybody was, I mean."

"You've got a smart grandmother," said Andy, turning up his own street.

"You'd better believe it," said Joe, walking backwards and waving good-bye. "She's full of smarts." Then he hurried on home.

"Molly ole boy!" he cried as he came up to the house. "Want to come inside? Molly ole—hey, where is she?"

"She's walking around," said Grandmother, coming out the door. "She's getting her exercise. You don't think she just sits on those eggs 24 hours a day, do you?

5. See Psalm 80 also.

"Will she remember to come back?" said Joe. "She won't get lost, will she?"

"No—she's just around the side of the house. Want me to help you carry her coop inside while she's not in it?" They picked it up, very gently, and carried it in between them, Joe walking backwards and looking over his shoulder. They settled the precious cargo in the corner. Then Joe went out and sat on the doorstep and waited for Molly to come back.

"She'll come back," said Grandmother. "You don't have to watch."

"She might not have a sense of direction," said Joe. "I don't want to have to sit on those eggs myself. Besides I'm getting rather fond of her."

Molly ole boy came back and settled carefully on her little brood-to-be. There was a fluttering inside the eggs now, warm against her feathery stomach.

Joe told Grandmother the story of the vineyard while he was doing his kitchen chores and she was getting their evening meal. Sure enough, Grandmother was full of smarts.

"Sure," she said. "Our prophet Isaiah speaks of Israel as a vineyard too.[6] It's easy to see why the Temple priests and religious leaders stalked off. They knew who they were in that story."

"Who *were* they?" said Joe.

"Why they were the wicked farmers!" said Grandmother.

"Oh, sure," said Joe. "Why didn't I get that?"

"The farmers take care of the vines. The religious leaders take care of us. At least they're supposed to," Grandmother said, beating her batter a little harder at that point.

"But who were the landowner's servants? The chaps the wicked farmers killed?"

"Think about it." That's all she would say.

Halfway through the meal, Joe still hadn't guessed. "All right, I give up," he said at last. "Who *were* the servants?"

Grandmother spread honey on a biscuit. "All right," she said. "All down through the years God has sent His prophets to warn people

6. See Isaiah 5:1,2.

of their sins. The prophets were His servants, weren't they?"

"You mean the guys the wicked farmers beat up and treated so badly were God's prophets?"

"Sure they were," said Grandmother. "God sent His prophets to the Israelites. And how did the Israelites treat them? How did the *leaders* treat them?"

Joe couldn't answer. He sat thinking and munching.

"Well, take Jeremiah," prodded[7] Grandmother. "God sent Jeremiah to warn the people of their sins, and what did the leaders do to him?"

"Beat him up, I guess. And put him in prison."

"They sure did," said Grandmother. "He was arrested several times—and whipped—and kept in a prison dungeon. And worse!"

"Worse?" said Joe.

"Yes. He was lowered into a pit. And he sank—"

"Oh I remember!" said Joe. "He sank into the wet slimy clay at the bottom! Yaaak. They clobbered him all right."

"Well then," said Grandmother, "let's have a countdown. We can check them off, one at a time. The landowner was God—"

"The vineyard was Israel—"

"And the farmers were the religious leaders—"

"And the servants were God's prophets—"

"And the son—"

"The son was God's Son—the Messiah!" shouted Joe. He was just dipping some bread in the gravy in the big bowl at the center of the table. When it struck him, he almost dropped the bread in. "Then if Jesus *is* the Messiah—He was talking about Himself! And some say He is. The Messiah, I mean."

"Ohhhhhhhhhh, mercy, no," said Grandmother. "That's impossible. Nobody's killed *Him.* He's still alive. He's very much alive. If He *is* the Messiah He'll set up His kingdom right here, and rescue us from the Roman rule." She munched her biscuit. "I don't know how He could be," she finished.

Joe mopped up the rest of his gravy. Grandmother was probably

7. Like "poked."

44

right; she usually was. She was sure full of smarts to figure out that whole story. They finished their meal in silence.

The silence settled down over the little house. The evening sacrifice was over now, had been over now for some time. They'd been so busy talking they hadn't noticed.

The psalm had been sung—

> "Stand up, O God, and judge the earth
> For all of it belongs to you. . . ."

And the lamb had been slain.

Molly had her head tucked in her feathers, and had pulled her eyelids up over her eyes like a blanket. The eggs were silent and mysterious under her body, warm with promise. . . .

# Chapter Seven

# WEDNESDAY

The morning burst out like a great explosion.

One of the priests climbed up to a high point of the Temple and looked out over the east.

Everyone waited.

Then, "The morning shines already!" he called back.

"Does it light up the sky as far as Hebron?" the captain asked.

"Yea—as far as Hebron!"

That was the signal for the orders to fly.

"Bring in the lamb to be slain!"

"Open the gates of the Temple!"

"Blow the trumpets!"

And the trumpets blew and the sun burst forth all the way, lighting the gold and the white marble of the Temple until it shone in dazzling beauty.

And the choirs burst forth too, with the psalm that was always sung on the fourth day—

> "O Lord God
>     To whom vengeance belongs. . . ."

The air was still and clear, and the music resounded all over

Jerusalem. Grandmother heard it and bolted out of bed. Molly heard it and jerked her eyelid blankets down from her eyes quickly, and ruffled her feathers and raised herself up from her eggs. The unborn chicks seemed to hear it too, and fluttered in their shells. Joe heard it, sat up on his mat—and lay back down again quickly, hoping Grandmother would think he was still asleep.

---

"Come on, Joe. Up, up and away. We've got to clean the house for the Passover!"

Good grief. She'd seen him.

"We've *been* cleaning the house!" he groaned.

"Well there's a bit more to do," she said. "Get bustling."

"We've been bustling for days, Grandmother!"

"Well some people have been getting ready for weeks!"

It was true. Such housecleaning you never saw in your life. The houses were almost turned inside out. Everything in them was scrubbed and the floors were swept and swept and swept again. Even the usual cooking utensils were put away. Only special dishes, brought out lovingly once a year, were used for the Passover meal. No bread with leaven[1] in it was allowed in the house, either.

"Why?" said Joe.

"Because when the Israelites left Egypt, they left in such a hurry they didn't have time to make bread with yeast in it."

"I know that," said Joe. "But sometimes I wonder why we're still doing it after all these years."

"We'll do it and do it and do it again—until the Messiah comes," said Grandmother firmly.

And so they prepared for the feast to come. There were bitter herbs to remind them of their suffering in Egypt. And the unleavened bread. And then of course the Passover lamb that was killed and eaten, to remind them of that dreadful night when the angel of death *passed over* all the homes that had blood sprinkled on the doors.

1. That's yeast.

Every year Joe asked about it. And every year Grandmother told him. They never tired of talking about it. Joe's Uncle Simon and Aunt Rachel and their children were all coming for the Passover meal. For there had to be at least ten people for the meal with the Passover lamb.

Molly's coop was carried out in the yard again. She fussed and squawked and ruffled her feathers as she walked alongside Joe and Grandmother, scolding them in fury and concern for her brood. Molly was getting quite nippy these days.

"When are you going to have those crazy chicks, Molly ole boy?" Joe said.

"Waaauk puk puk!" she snapped back.

"What do you mean, you can't manage it yet?" Joe said. "Concentrate, ole boy, concentrate."

"WaaaaAUUK!"

"Well I'm tired of waiting," Joe said.

Molly glared at him, as if to say, "And how do you think *I* feel?"

"Don't tease her," said Grandmother. "She's weary sitting on those eggs."

"I'm going to call her Mrs. Wearybottom," Joe said. Molly squawked again, louder.

"Well, you are supposed to have them this week. And here it is Wednesday. And you haven't even got started."

Molly stalked off, muttering in her feathers.

Grandmother laughed. "I think she knows what you're saying."

"There was something else He said yesterday," Joe said, "but I can't remember what it was."

"Who?" said Grandmother.

"My friend. Jesus of Nazareth."

"I thought we were talking about Molly."

Joe had stopped in his tracks and was just staring. He'd forgotten all about Molly. What was it that Jesus had said? He'd ask Andy.

"You'll have to go out in the hills and gather me a sack of thorns for my fire," Grandmother was saying. "But first you'll have to take my dough downtown to the baker's oven and get it baked. We'll need plenty of unleavened bread to last through the week. And I can't bake it all in my oven here."

"Is it all right if Andy goes with me?" Joe said.

"It's all right if his mother will let him out," said Grandmother. "They have plenty to do. They're getting ready for Passover too.

---

It seemed hours before Joe was finished with all his chores. But at last he was on his way to the baker's ovens with his basket of bread dough. He and Andy were fighting the crowds again.

"They have a lot of dough in there," Joe said to Andy as he came out the baker's. "It'll be a long time before they get to ours. We can go over to the Temple and pick the bread up on our way back."

"Do you think Jesus of Nazareth will be there?" said Andy.

"That's what I'm hoping," said Joe. And they both quickened their pace.

"EeeeAUUUH" said a donkey in Joe's ear.

"EeeeAUUUH yourself," said Joe laughing, as he pushed the donkey gently aside. He thought of the donkey Jesus had ridden on, and wondered where it had gone.

Inside the Court of the Gentiles was the same mad scramble. People from everywhere, every country, every province. Joe and Andy looked all over in the courts where they were allowed, and peeked into the courts where they weren't. They looked on Solomon's Porch, too, but Jesus wasn't anywhere to be found. "I wanted to see Him," said Joe. "I really wanted to see Him. I wanted to get close enough to talk to Him. I really wanted—"

They stopped short.

The man ahead of them had stumbled and fallen. It set up quite a commotion. People stopped so quickly that they bumped heads for yards back. For no one would help him. People spread out as best they could and walked around him. Joe and Andy were pressed back, elbows in their faces.

One tall man, his head in the sky, his nose in the air, drew his fine robes around him, and hanging onto his prayer shawl, kept such a distance that Joe and Andy were pressed into the crowd clean out of sight. They were lost in a tangle of robes and animals and smells, and it was a few seconds before they found each other again.

At last the man gathered his packages from the ground and scrambled painfully to his feet.

"Phew!" said Joe. "Why didn't somebody help him?"

"That holy man with the prayer box didn't even want to touch him," said Andy.

"He's one of the Pharisees," said Joe. "One of the religious leaders. He didn't want to get himself defiled. The guy was a foreigner."

"Was he a Samaritan?" Every Jewish boy knew that the Jews would have nothing to do with the Samaritans. They wouldn't even go through Samaria. They'd travel around it, as if it were full of measles.

And why?

Because the Samaritans were half Jewish and half heathen. It was partly a racial problem. And partly because many generations ago, the Samaritans heckled the Jews when they were trying to rebuild Jerusalem's walls.[2] And the Jews were still "all bent out of shape" about it.

"Did you hear the story that Jesus told about the Good Samaritan?" said Joe.

"What's good about a Samaritan?"

"Well, some lawyer was asking Jesus what love was all about, and Jesus told him that we should love our neighbors. So the lawyer asked who *was* his neighbor. And Jesus told this story."

They made their way along Solomon's Porch, then headed toward a gate. It didn't look as if Jesus of Nazareth was going to be there after all. "Anyhow," Joe said when they got back out on the street, "there was this Samaritan traveling from Jerusalem to Jericho."

"He was in trouble right there," said Andy. The road from Jerusalem to Jericho was a winding one, lined with spooky caves and

2. See Nehemiah for story.

infested[3] with robbers. Anyone who traveled that road alone was either very brave or very foolish.

"No—he wasn't in trouble, but somebody was. Anyhow, he was going along this spooky road. And suddenly—he stopped his donkey." Joe stopped, going through the motions. "Lying alongside the road was a man—beaten to a pulp."

"Dead?"

"The Samaritan didn't know. But he got off his donkey—" Joe swung his leg up and over as if he were getting off a donkey.

"Is this for real?" said Andy.

Joe hadn't heard him. He was wrapped up in his tale now. "And he went over—and he saw that this man was wounded—badly. And he turned him over on his back. And he gave him first aid." Joe went through the motions, intent on his task. "And he told him not to worry; everything was under control. Then he got his donkey alongside, real close, and—hup!—slung the wounded man over it." Joe struggled with his imaginary load.

"Didn't the wounded man have a donkey of his own?" Andy wanted to know.

"Not in this story, he didn't," said Joe. "The Samaritan took him to the next inn. And there he put him in a room, and took care of him all through the night."

"Wow," Andy was impressed.

"And in the morning the Samaritan paid the bill and left more money for the wounded man's care. 'Take care of him until I come back,' he said. 'And if it costs more, I'll pay it.'" Joe imitated the Samaritan's voice.

"Wooooeeee," said Andy.

They were silent for a moment. And then, "Is that all there is to the story?" said Andy. "What does that have to do with who's your neighbor?"

"That's the point," said Joe. "The Samaritan did not pass the man by. But the man had been lying there a long time and two other people *had* passed him by."

3. It was swarming with them; they were all over the place.

51

"Two?" said Andy, horrified. "Who?"

"One was a Jewish priest. And the other was a Jewish Temple assistant."[4]

"Ohhh, boy."

"Yup. They didn't just pass him by. They crossed over to the other side of the road so they wouldn't even have to go *near* him."

"Why'd they do that?"

"Well, after all, they were serving in the Temple. Didn't want to defile themselves. The man might be dead."

"So they just left the poor guy there?"

"They left the poor guy there."

They thought about it for a minute.

"So the wounded man was the Samaritan's neighbor. Is that it?"

"*Anybody's* your neighbor if he needs help. *That's* it. That's what Jesus was saying."

"So I shouldn't look down my nose at anybody if he needs help?"

"That's the general idea."

"Then we should have helped that man up," said Andy.

"We couldn't," said Joe. "We got pushed out of the way." And then, "But maybe we should have tried harder."

They were by the gate by this time. "I have to gather thorn branches for my grandmother's fire," Joe said. "Do you want to come with me?"

"Why not?" Andy said.

"We can get the bread on the way back. Do you think you could carry the bread while I carry my sack of thorns? Or you carry my sack of thorns and I'll carry the bread."

"You carry the bread *and* the sack of thorns—and I'll carry you," said Andy.

They both laughed.

The traffic was heavy on the road outside, but they began to run, darting in and out between people and donkeys, chasing each other and laughing, until they were out of breath. Then they began to walk again.

4. He was a Levite. He served in the Temple and sang in the choir.

"Molly ole boy have her chicks yet?" Andy said.

"No, not yet," said Joe. "And she's pretty nippy about it. She flies into a rage if I get near her."

"Well, it probably is pretty boring to be sitting on twenty eggs day after da—"

Andy stopped suddenly, staring at two men who were coming toward them. "Those men," he said, "they're a couple of His disciples. I've seen them before."

"Then where is He? Where is Jesus?"

"I thought He was in Bethany," said Andy.

"Maybe He's up in the Mount of Olives," said Joe. "Shall we ask?"

But the two men were passing by now, talking earnestly: they did not as much as glance at the boys. Soon they were past, and the opportunity was gone. Joe's heart was beating fast. "I'll bet that's where He is now," he said, "and I'll bet they're coming down to buy food. The big guy was Peter. He's the strongest and bravest." They were walking backwards now, looking at the backs of the two men, Joe tripping over his sack. "And the other one is John." Then they remembered their errand, and went off the road to gather the thorns. They filled the sack quickly and started back into Jerusalem through the east gate that opened into the Temple area. They darted expertly through the crowd, Andy going ahead to clear the way for Joe and his sack.

It was while they were still in the Temple area that they saw the other disciple. Joe saw him first. His head was down and he was hurrying, his eyes intent on the ground.

"Which one is he?" hissed Andy. "Do you know him?"

"I don't know him," said Joe. "But I heard someone call him by name."

They were at the bakery by then, and Joe darted in, picked up Grandmother's bread, and they hurried on toward home. Joe left Andy at his corner and got home in time for Molly's feeding. "Have you wasted another day?" he said. But Molly wasn't speaking to him.

"Did you see Jesus of Nazareth down at the Temple?" Grandmother wanted to know.

"No," said Joe. "We looked all over for Him. We heard He didn't go back to Bethany either. We don't know where He went. We think He's up in the Mount of Olives."

"Why do you say that?"

"Well. We saw two of His disciples coming down. I know one of them. His name is Peter. We think they were coming down to buy food."

"Speaking of food," said Grandmother, "we don't need any more bread. Uncle Simon and Aunt Rachel will bring some. They have ovens dug in the ground in their yard. But you'll have to get some water. Now."

"Can't we borrow from the neighbors?" said Joe.

"They hardly have enough for themselves," said Grandmother. "We'll get our own. Now get on with you."

Joe took the pitcher she handed him and darted away.

"Who is my neighbor?" he called back.

"What's that?"

"Don't you know that *anybody* is your neighbor—if he's in trouble?"

He left her with her mouth open.

"Grandmother thinks I've gone bananas,"[5] he thought. "I'll have to explain that to her when I get back."

And he did.

He told her the story of the Good Samaritan. And more about the two disciples they'd met on the road. And about the disciple they'd seen in the Temple area.

"He looked funny, Grandmother," he said.

"What do you mean, funny?"

"Well not funny. He looked strange. If he wasn't a disciple I'd say he looked sneaky."

"*Sneaky?*"

"Well, as if he didn't want anybody to see him."

---

5. In those days he probably would have said "gone figs." They didn't grow bananas.

55

"Did you say you knew him?"

"I don't know him, Grandmother. But I heard somebody call him by his name."

"And? What was it?"

"I can't remember."

---

That night, lying on his mat, Joe wondered where Jesus of Nazareth was sleeping. At Bethany? Or was He sleeping out under the stars on the Mount of Olives? With all of His disciples with Him?

"Good night, Molly ole boy," he called out in the dark.

Molly didn't bother to answer.

But Grandmother did.

"Go to sleep, Joseph," she said.

But he sat bolt upright in bed, instead. For suddenly he remembered.

"Grandmother!"

"Yes?"

"I remember that other disciple's name. The one who looked as if he didn't want anybody to see him."

"Well?"

"It was Judas."

# Chapter Eight

# THURSDAY

"The morning shines already!"

"Open the gates of the Temple!"

"Slay the lamb!"

"Blow the trumpets!"

Joe sat bolt upright in bed. Molly was glaring at him. "Have you been sitting there staring at me all night?" he said. "And where are the chicks?" She turned her head away, then got off her nest and stalked toward the door.

But nothing could dampen Joe's mood this morning. Uncle Simon and Aunt Rachel were coming, and all the children. For the great day was here at last. The day of the Feast of the Passover.

"Let's get her coop out while she's off her nest," said Grandmother. And they did. It was out to stay this time. No chicken coops allowed in the house on Passover day. Joe and Grandmother scurried about all morning, doing last-minute chores. Grandmother checked the list—herbs, unleavened bread—Uncle Simon would go to the Temple and buy the lamb when he came.[1] She polished the chests and benches until they shone, and fluffed up the pillows.

---

1. The head of the household always went to the Temple, had a lamb killed, and brought it home to be cooked.

By noon, everything was ready. Inside, the house was shining, smelling faintly of herbs and smoke. Outside the air was clear and chilly. It had turned cold in the night. The sky was cloudless. Joe did a last-minute cleanup job outside. "Watch it," he teased Molly as he walked past, "or you'll wind up some night in a stew."

"*Joseph!*" Grandmother was behind him, scolding. But her eyes were smiling.

They had a hasty lunch. And then the dishes were carefully washed and put away, until after the Passover. And the special Passover dishes were brought out.

And then—

With whoops and shouts and much merriment, Uncle Simon and Aunt Rachel and the children descended upon them. There were kisses and hugs and slaps and thumps on the backs, and everyone talking at once.

"My how you've grown!"

"It's good to see you!"

"You've been working too hard, Simon—you look thin!"

"It's good for me!"

"And how's your hen?" said Uncle Simon to Joe.

"You mean Molly ole boy?"

"Ha! Is *that* what you named her?" Uncle Simon roared with laughter. "Has she had her chicks yet?"

"Waaaaaaauk puk puk puk!" came from Molly's coop, as if she were saying, "Oh, good grief—not that again. Get off my back."

And so there was fussing and clucking and laughing and getting children settled and unpacking the donkey they'd brought along. And all the noises and smells went with them as they piled into the house.

"Mother, you're coming to live with us when summer's done," said Uncle Simon. "It's not fitting for you to be here alone."

"She's not alone!" Joe bellowed. "I'm with her!"

There was an argument about that, but it was a good-natured one. And then the children were settled and Aunt Rachel and Grandmother were on the doorstep talking and Joe and Uncle Simon went off to the Temple to buy the lamb and have it killed.

58

It was no problem getting through the crowded streets and across the Court of the Gentiles this time. Uncle Simon was tall and strong and walked ahead. And Joe just whipped into the holes he left behind.

Joe stood thrilled and trembling as he watched Uncle Simon put his hand on the lamb and hand it to the priest to be killed. He transferred the sins of the family to the lamb. And the lamb was killed in their place. Joe knew it all by heart.

On the way to the Temple, Joe had told Uncle Simon all he knew about Jesus of Nazareth. He was surprised to find that Uncle Simon knew all about Him too. The gossip got around. "Oh, yes," Uncle Simon said, "He's been healing the sick and the crippled all over the country. He healed a blind man in Jericho just before He got to Bethany on His way here. And of course you know it was in Bethany where He raised that man from the dead, a few months back."

"Lazarus?"

"Yes. Lazarus. Everybody knows about that."

"Does everybody believe it?" said Joe.

"Well those who have seen Lazarus alive believe it."

"Does everybody think He's the Messiah, Uncle Simon?"

"There are a lot of people who do think so."

"Do you?"

"Think He might be around today?" said Uncle Simon. "We might have a look."

Joe said nothing. Uncle Simon did not believe. And he didn't want to talk about it.

They looked around in all the courts where they were allowed. They looked on Solomon's Porch, too, but there was no Jesus.

He was gone.

"There was something that He said once," Joe said, "when He was teaching in the Temple, but I can't remember what it was."

"Does it matter?" said Uncle Simon.

"Well, I keep saying it doesn't matter. But it *does* matter. It keeps coming back. I keep thinking it was important. But I just can't remember it."

"Well. We'd better get on home. The women will want to cook this lamb right away."

When they got back to the house, the women had the fire going. The special utensils were all out, and the smell of herbs was in the air.

Joe went outside and whittled. The children were too small to play with. He poked around and found a branch and cut it down to size.

If Jesus of Nazareth was not at the Temple, where was He? Was He getting ready for the Passover Feast? Who would cook it for Him? Where would He eat it? Joe whittled away, scowling, lost in his thoughts.

———————————————

Joe didn't know it, but about a mile away Jesus of Nazareth's disciples were asking Him the same question. "Where do you want us to go," they said, "to prepare the Passover?"

"Go into Jerusalem," He said. "And as soon as you enter, you'll see a man walking, carrying a pitcher of water."

A *man?* Carrying a pitcher of water? Men didn't carry water. Only women carried water. A man carrying water would certainly be easy to spot.

"Follow this man. He will enter a house. Follow him in. And say to the man who lives there, 'Our Master says for you to show us the room where He will eat the Passover Feast with His disciples.' He will take you upstairs to a large upper room. That's the place. Just go ahead and prepare the meal there." He nodded toward the two of them.

The two of them started off. They were the same two the boys had run into the day before, Peter and John. They hurried off to Jerusalem, talking all the way, about what was uppermost in their minds. It was not, *would* Jesus set up His kingdom, but *when*. They were absolutely sure He was going to do it. It never entered their minds that He wouldn't. Of course He would. That's what the whole thing was all about. Everybody knew that. Well, they hashed it over for the umpteenth time, right up to until they got to the gate at

Jerusalem. And before they had time to ask themselves "Where is he?" they saw him. Sure enough. Carrying a pitcher of water.

Astonishing!

Didn't the man feel foolish? Men didn't carry pitchers of water. He didn't look as if he felt foolish. As a matter of fact, he didn't even look foolish, and nobody paid any attention to him. Peter and John followed him a cautious distance behind until he went into a house. Then, a little embarrassed they went in too, and asked for the man of the house—and said what Jesus had told them to.

And he didn't look surprised. He simply led them upstairs—and there it was. It was a huge room, and nicely furnished. There was a long table set, and everything they needed was there. All they had to do was get things in order and get the meal on the table.

---

Joe stopped his whittling and went off to see what Uncle Simon was doing. He found him a few houses away, talking solemnly to some other men. Joe stood a respectful distance away and listened. They were talking grown-up talk, way over his head. Taxes and troubles and the misery of being under Roman rule and how wonderful it would be if the Messiah God had promised would come and set up His kingdom and set them all free. Their voices were solemn and low, for this was the Passover time.

There was a strange mixture of feelings about Passover time. It was solemn, and yet somehow there was a sort of holiday spirit in the air. And there was a longing for the Messiah.

Right in the middle of all the talking, all the men seemed to look up at the sky at once, as if on signal. There was a chill in the air now. It was almost time for sunset. Uncle Simon and Joe hurried back to the house. Joe fed Molly quickly outside; they had nothing to say to each other. Then he hurried into the house and joined the confusion of getting the children settled on the cushions around the low table. It was finally straightened out as to who would sit where; everyone was in his place. And the meal was put on the table.

A perfect lamb.

No bent ear.
No crooked leg.
No weak eyes.
No crooked tail.
No defects—not even a little one.
A lamb without blemish—absolutely nothing wrong with it.
There were stacks of unleavened bread[2] and a huge bowl of bitter herbs, and wine.

They bowed their heads, and Uncle Simon thanked God for their meal. In the distance they could hear the music from the Temple for the evening sacrifice—

"Sing aloud unto God our strength—"[3]

_____

They were shut away from the cold evening air, snug and cozy. Grandmother's fire was burning briskly, the smoke curling against the ceiling and escaping out of the windows. And the odor of roast lamb and herbs filled the air. While they ate, they remembered the blood of the lamb that was sprinkled on the doorposts of the Israelites' homes to save them from punishment—back in Egypt so many, many years ago.

Joe felt solemn as he looked around the table at the little children, so much smaller than he. And quite grown up. He would be a man soon. Then *he* would stand around in groups with other men, talking about the Messiah to come. And taxes. And all the other things he didn't understand now. He looked at Grandmother and Aunt Rachel and Uncle Simon and all the rest of them—his very own family. "I like this home," he thought. "I like it." He missed the good bread Grandmother baked, and the honey. The unleavened bread was flat and tasteless and hard to swallow. Yaaauk, he thought. As he ate it he wondered where Jesus was eating. Where was He now, right now, this moment? He really ought to be in a palace,

2. Without yeast, remember?
3. See Psalm 81.

Joe thought, eating the Passover. A *king's* palace. That's where He ought to be.

---

Jesus looked around the long table at His disciples, in the borrowed upper room. "I've looked forward to this hour with you," He said. "I've looked forward to it with deep longing. I've been anxious to eat this Passover meal with you before My suffering begins."

"Suffering?" they said. They looked up from their eating quickly.

And then He dropped the bombshell.

"I am serious when I tell you this," He said. "One of you will betray Me."

They all stopped eating.

"Who? *Who?* WHO?"

"It is one of you sitting right here with Me," He said. "I told you before that I would be betrayed."

"But we didn't believe You! Who is it?"

"Is it I?"

"Am I the one?"

"Or I?"

"Or I?"

Even Judas said it.

"Am I the one?"

Jesus dipped a piece of bread into the gravy, and handed it to Judas. "Hurry. What you must do, do quickly," He said.

And Judas hurried out.

Do *what* now?

Pay for the meal?

Yes, that must be it. Pay for the meal, they thought. Judas was the treasurer.

So they all started talking again.

Betray Jesus?

One of them? One of His own disciples? Impossible!

Even though He'd said it, not one of them believed it.

They went back to their eating.

And as they were eating, Jesus took a small piece of the bread.

And He blessed it. And He broke it apart, in pieces. And He gave a piece to each of them. "Take it," He said, "and eat it. For this represents My body, given for you."

They sat staring at Him, each one holding his piece of bread in his hand.

And then He took a cup of wine. And He gave thanks for that. And He gave it to them. "Pass it around," He said. "Each of you, drink from it. For this represents My blood that shall be poured out—to forgive the sins of multitudes."

They began to eat their bread and drink the wine. And wondered. What did He mean? It had always been a *lamb's* blood poured out for forgiveness of sins.

"Eat the bread and drink the wine in remembrance of Me," He said softly.

They were very solemn and thoughtful for a few moments.

But only for a few moments.

Then they began to talk again. And of all things—they began to argue among themselves as to who would have the highest rank in the coming kingdom!

As to Jesus' being betrayed—they'd already forgotten about it.

They hadn't really believed it anyhow.

-------

But Judas had believed it.

For indeed it *had* been Judas the boys had seen on Wednesday in the Temple. And if he had looked to them as if he was up to no good, it was because he *was* up to no good. He had even then been on his way to the religious leaders. He knew that they wanted to arrest Jesus, but not in a public place. They were afraid of a riot; they wanted to arrest Him secretly, when He was away from the crowd. And they'd been looking for someone to turn Him in.

Judas was their man.

He'd made a deal with them that day.

He would turn Jesus in—

For thirty pieces of silver.

At the right time.

And in the right place.

Where they could arrest Him privately.

It was cold outside now. Judas wrapped his robe around him and headed for the house of the high priest.

---

Grandmother and Aunt Rachel were cleaning up after the Passover meal. The older children were getting drowsy; the smaller ones were already asleep. There was the rustle and bustle of getting all the extra mats laid out and getting everybody tucked off to sleep in the proper places. But at last it was done.

The last thing Joe did was to go out and cover Molly's coop with a part of an old blanket. It was cold outside now, very cold. She was asleep and did not stir. Joe was glad to get back in the house.

The grown-ups stayed up and talked by the light of the one lamp left lighted. Joe was allowed to stay up too. He tried to listen but his mind wasn't on it. Their voices seemed to come from far away.

Where was Jesus now? And who was He with?

A strange feeling of uneasiness came over Joe, a feeling he couldn't put his finger on.

Was it fear?

He didn't know.

Was this what Grandmother meant when she said she "had a feeling in her bones" that something was going to happen?

And her bones twanged?

Joe's heart began to beat just a little faster.

And his breathing was shaky.

His bones twanged too.

# Chapter Nine

# THURSDAY- LATER

Joe plunged into the wildest sort of dreaming.

At first he dreamed in little bits and pieces.

First he dreamed he was in Uncle Simon's vineyard. And he overheard the other workers plotting to kill the owner's son when he came to collect the rent. He laid aside his hoe and sneaked away. Once he was out of sight he ran to find Uncle Simon. But Uncle Simon was nowhere to be found. Joe ran madly in every direction. He never found Uncle Simon. And the owner's son never came. That dream ended up a deadend street.

And then he dreamed he was at a dinner party. And the dinner party seemed to go on forever—people coming and going, as they did at parties back in those days. Neighbors came in, beggars stood outside the door, and onlookers stood against the wall, gawking; it was the custom. In the dream, Joe was one of the onlookers. He stood against the wall, right opposite the guest of honor. And the guest of honor was—Jesus of Nazareth Himself. And then Joe saw that it was Passover food they were eating. There were the bitter herbs and the bread without yeast. But there wasn't any lamb.

67

"Where's the lamb?" he tried to cry out, but nothing came—not even a whisper.

"Where's the lamb?" he tried again. But only a squeak came out, and no one heard him. Then he saw that Jesus was looking right at him. "Where's the lamb?" he tried to say. And they looked at each other. And then—

"Joseph Simon Bar-Jason," Jesus said. Jesus of Nazareth knew Joe's name!

And then suddenly, in his dream, Joe felt that Jesus not only knew his name, but He knew *him*, Joe, everything about him. Where he was born and what he thought and how he felt—just *everything*.

And it seemed as if the two of them were all alone in the room. No one else was paying any attention to them.

"Where's the lamb?" Joe said. "I want to know."

He sat bolt upright in bed. "Where's the lamb?" he said in the dark. And he realized he'd been dreaming. He was damp with sweat, and his nightshirt clung to him.

"Joe?" whispered Grandmother. "Are you all right?"

"Yes," he whispered back, getting to his feet. "I just thought I heard Molly. I'm going to get a drink of water, and check her out."

Grandmother didn't answer, and Joe got to his feet and picked his way through the humps of sleeping children at his end of the room, and found his way to the door. There was a buttery moon outside and the air was cold. He got his drink and picked his way back to his mat. By the time he had curled up and squinched himself into a little ball to sleep again, he'd almost forgotten what his dream had been all about. It was about midnight. A cloud came over the moon and the little room was darker now.

---

The long shadows stretched over Jerusalem, beyond its gates, and settled in its dark ravines, stretching up to the western slopes of the Mount of Olives. Almost all the lights were out now. The Passover feasts were ended and the streets were deserted. Everyone seemed to be settled down for the night.

Well, almost.

The lights were on in the house of Caiaphas, the High Priest, and his father-in-law Annas. And in the Fortress of Antonia where the Roman governor Pilate had made his headquarters. And here and there in the dark there were people bustling about.

Temple guards,

Roman soldiers,

And the religious leaders of the Temple.

Up on the Mount of Olives, in a garden called Gethsemane, Jesus and His disciples had gone for the night. It was a walled garden, and in it was a grove of olive trees. It was quiet and private, and they'd gone there many times before. They did not go to the garden this night to sleep, however. For as they had left the Upper room and wound their way up here there was a strange sense of "happening" in the air, and the disciples knew that there would be little sleep for them tonight. The mystery was almost unbearable.

What was going on?

"How brief are these moments, before I must go away and leave you," Jesus had told them. "And though you search for Me, you cannot come to Me. So I'm leaving you with a new commandment. Love each other—just as much as I love you."

"Where are You going?" they had wanted to know. And He had said, "You can't go with Me now. But you'll follow Me later."

"But why can't I come now," Peter had sputtered, "I'm ready to die for You."

"No—" Jesus had said—"tonight all of you will desert Me."

"Never!" This from Peter. "I'll never desert You no matter what the others do!"

But Jesus had said, "Peter, let me tell you something. Between now and tomorrow morning when the rooster crows, you will deny Me three times. You'll deny you even know Me."

And Peter had exploded. "No! NO! Even if I have to die, I'll never deny You!"

"Nor I!" the others had said. "Nor I. Nor I!" Their voices filled the Upper room.

All that had happened a couple of hours ago.

And now they were in the garden.

And their heads were spinning with questions.

*What was going on?*

Would someone take Jesus away?

What nonsense!

Of course He would resist.

He was the Messiah.

He was here to set up His kingdom.

And of course they would help Him. Wasn't that what it was all about?

Peter was still muttering in his beard about not denying Him. He'd stick with Him to the end. The others were thinking much the same thing. There would be something adventurous about helping Him set up His kingdom. Such derring-do!

Jesus' voice interrupted their thoughts. "Sit here while I go and pray," He said. He took three of His disciples[1] with Him, a little farther into the grove of olive trees, and asked them to wait. And then He went still farther in, and began to pray—

—alone.

While some of the disciples were whispering among themselves and some were snoozing—Jesus was alone, talking to God.

His Father.

"Whatever You want to do," He said, "will be done—"

And so the hardest choice and the greatest choice in all the world was made. And it set in motion the great drama that followed.

Nothing could be changed now.

And no one could turn back.

Jesus of Nazareth had made His choice.

And the disciples were asleep when it happened—the choice that changed the lives of all of them, and of Joe and of Grandmother and Uncle Simon and Aunt Rachel and the children—

And Andy—

And countless[2] other people in Jerusalem—

And the surrounding countries—

1. Peter, James and John.
2. Too many to be counted.

And all over the world.
Not just that night—
And not just that year,
But for all the years to follow,
Two thousand of them,
And more—as long as the world exists.

It was late now—very late. Jesus came back to where all the disciples were waiting—some of them talking, some of them snoozing.

And then—

What was this?

What had been faint noises that blended with the night noises of insects and stirring leaves became a scuffling of feet getting closer. And what had been faint lights quivering far away and unimportant, became torches and lanterns—many of them, close, and closer.

It all seemed to burst at once upon the quiet of the garden—

The Temple police,

And armed men,

And Judas.

The disciples scrambled to their feet, still half asleep. They were dazed and unbelieving in the sudden glare of the lights.

No one spoke for a minute, and then—

"Who are you looking for?"

It was Jesus speaking.

"Jesus of Nazareth!" The answer came back from behind the blazing lights, sharp as the crack of a whip. The disciples were still dumbfounded. Not one of them could find his tongue.

And then, "I am He," Jesus said.

And as He said it, a sudden shock of power seemed to split the air like lightning, and the Temple police and the armed men and Judas all staggered backward as if they'd been zapped—

And fell to the ground!

Now no ordinary man, however great, could have done this simply by saying, "I am He." This was something bigger than human, bigger than anything they had ever experienced. It was like when Moses, so many many years ago had said to God, "Who'll I tell them *sent* me?" And God had answered—

"Tell them I AM sent you."

In some strange way it seemed as if Jesus had just said the same thing.

I AM.

And a great and terrible power had filled the air.

If THIS didn't prove that He was the Messiah, the disciples thought, nothing ever would. NOW He would take charge and set everything straight. The disciples stood there in shock, waiting for something terrific to happen.

But nothing did.

Jesus simply said again, "Whom are you searching for?"

"Jesus of Nazareth," they said again, staggering to their feet.

"I am the One you are looking for," He said calmly. "Let the rest of these men go."

Now they were poking Judas, pushing him forward, to do as he had promised. They wanted to make sure they got the right man. Judas didn't need any poking, however. He came straight up to Jesus. "Master!" he said. And he embraced Him and kissed Him on the cheek.

For one brief moment Jesus looked at Judas. Then, "Judas," He said, "how can you do this? Betray the Messiah with a kiss!"

The disciples stood with their mouths open.

Judas!

He had not left the Upper room to pay for the meal. He had left to turn Jesus in!

Good *grief!* Was it *possible?*

Yes it was indeed.

The mob started forward now, toward Jesus.

And the disciples were galvanized[3] into action.

"Master!" they cried, "shall we fight?"

Then, with a sudden burst of courage, Peter drew his sword and— Whop!

Slashed it through the air toward one of the high priest's servants.

Now Peter wasn't used to using a sword. He wasn't used to danger

3. Like they felt they had to so something.

72

either. In fact he wasn't very brave. He was paralyzed with fear. He slashed through the dark—and lopped off the servant's ear!

"No, Peter, no," said Jesus. "Don't resist any more."

He turned to the mob. "Am I some dangerous criminal," He said, "that you had to arm yourselves with swords and clubs before you could come for Me? I was with you at the Temple every day, teaching. You didn't stop Me then."

He didn't wait for them to answer. He turned to Peter again. "Put away your sword," He said. "Don't you realize I could ask My Father for thousands of angels to protect us and He would send them immediately? This all has to happen so that everything God said in the Scriptures would come to pass." And He reached out to the man whose ear had been lopped off. He touched the wound—

And the ear was instantly restored! It was just suddenly *there* again, as though it had never been lopped off!

Every man there stood dumbfounded. Things were happening too fast. No one could quite grasp yet what was going on.

"This is all happening," Jesus said again, "so that everything the prophets have said will come true."

An awful fear filled the air, and filled their hearts. The disciples began to back away, leaving Jesus standing there alone. Judas stepped aside. And the mob descended on Him.

The Temple police,

The armed men,

All of them.

And the bushes crackled as the disciples fled, stumbling into the night.

And the night wind sighed through the branches of the giant olive trees.

And Jesus stood, His hands hanging down by His sides, waiting.

# Chapter Ten

# FRIDAY MORNING

Arrested?!?

*Arrested??!!!!!?*

It couldn't be possible. Joe ran outside to where Uncle Simon and Grandmother were talking. "Who was arrested, Uncle Simon?" he cried, although he had already heard Uncle Simon say it. He had to hear it again.

"Jesus of Nazareth," said Uncle Simon.

Joe stood there paralyzed. At that moment if someone had built a fire under him, he couldn't have moved.

He had awakened this Friday morning to the distant sounds of the sacrifice at the Temple—

> "The Lord is King!
>     He is robed in majesty and strength . . .
>     The world is His throne. . . ."

Uncle Simon had already been up and away, to attend the morning worship at the Temple and to witness the sacrifice of the lamb. This was part of what he had come to Jerusalem for—to eat the evening Passover with his family and to worship at the Temple. Joe had followed Grandmother as she bustled about, tidying up, and he'd helped Aunt Rachel roll up their family's mats and tie them neatly at both ends. He'd helped her tie up their bundles of clothing too, and everything was stacked neatly, ready to get packed on the little donkey. For Uncle Simon and his family had to get back to their home in Hebron. And they had to get there before sunset, when the Sabbath would begin.[1] The children had been fed, but Grandmother and Aunt Rachel had waited breakfast for Uncle Simon to come back, so they could eat together. Joe had been allowed to wait too; he was almost grownup now.

And now Uncle Simon was back with this stunning news.[2]

"Jesus of Nazareth?" said Aunt Rachel. She had come running out of the house now, too, and was standing behind Joe, her hands on his shoulders. Uncle Simon nodded without saying anything. And then,

"My breakfast will be ruined," muttered Grandmother, rushing back into the house. Uncle Simon and Aunt Rachel followed. Joe made his legs move with a great effort, and followed too.

They sat around the breakfast that Grandmother had laid out. There were slabs of cheese and a steaming bowl of rice and herbs and broiled fish. And there were oranges and plump apricots. The only thing missing was Grandmother's delicious biscuits and honey; there was nothing but the flat tasteless bread without yeast. The figs and olives weren't out yet, and the grapes wouldn't be along till fall.

"When did it happen?" said Aunt Rachel, "and how?"

"It all happened after midnight," said Uncle Simon, "somewhere around two—three—this morning. I only know what I heard; everyone was gossiping about it."

"Where did they do it?" said Joe. "Where was He last night?"

"Up on the Mount of Olives," said Uncle Simon. "In a garden somewhere up there."

---

1. Traveling on the Sabbath was a no-no. Remember?
2. It bowled them over.

"I knew He'd go there," whispered Joe under his breath. Nobody answered him.

"Anyhow," said Uncle Simon, "the religious leaders in the Temple sent some Temple police. They went up there and arrested Him and brought Him down."

"How did they know where to find Him?" said Joe. "How did they know where He was? There must have been a spy. *Somebody* must have told them."

"Somebody did."

They all stopped eating at once and looked up at Uncle Simon. They didn't say a word, but the question was in their eyes. Who had done such a thing?

"One of His disciples," said Uncle Simon.

Joe dropped a slab of cheese he had in his hand.

"A chap by the name of Judas," said Uncle Simon, and went back to his eating. "He was one of them. That's what they said. That's what I heard."

"But I saw him," said Joe. "Andy and I saw him." They all turned to look at him, and he hurried on. "We didn't see him turn Jesus in, or anything like that. I just mean we saw him walking along. We passed him. He had his eyes on the ground. He didn't look happy. And we wondered where he was going."

"Hmmm," said Uncle Simon. "Well. I only know what I heard. They took Him to the high priest—Caiaphas. Well, first they took Him to Annas—Caiaphas' father-in-law. And he gave Him a pretty rough time. And then Annas sent Him to Caiaphas. By that time a lot of the chief priests had assembled. And they questioned Him again. Tried to find witnesses against Him. They gave Him a rough time, too. From what I heard it was more like a small riot than a questioning."

"Was it a riot?" said Joe.

"Well. I guess you could call it a difference of opinion—with injuries," said Uncle Simon, as he reached for more food.

"But His disciples!" said Joe. "They could have helped Him if they had been there. They're big strong men. We saw two of them coming down from Mount Olive the other day. Andy and I saw

78

them. We thought they were coming down to buy food. They were two we knew. Peter and John. I've talked to them both before. They're great men. They would have fought for Him. *All* of His disciples would have protected Him. Why was He up there alone?"

There was a little silence before Uncle Simon answered. And then finally, "He wasn't up there alone, Joe. His disciples were up there with Him."

Joe stared at his uncle. He could feel his heart pounding.

"They all ran away. It was every man for himself. They left Him alone."

"Even Peter?" Joe's eyes were pleading.

"The one they call Peter followed Him down the slopes. Along with John."

"Ah," said Joe. "Peter followed Him. Then I know everything's going to be all right. He'll have a witness. What happened, Uncle Simon?"

"Nothing, as far as I know," said Uncle Simon. "While Jesus was inside having a rough time, Peter was outside, waiting in the court-yard."

"That's more like it," said Joe. "That's what I would have done. I would have stuck with Him. I would have stuck with Him in case He needed me. So if anybody asked me, I could be a witness for Him."

Uncle Simon cleared his throat and decided not to answer. After a few minutes he said, "Well. We don't know yet how it will turn out. It's still going on. And meanwhile"—he looked toward Aunt Rachel—"we've got to get ready to go home."

There was the bustle of getting the donkey packed and getting the family together—and while Grandmother and Aunt Rachel were counting noses and getting the last-minute things together, Uncle Simon took Joe aside for a minute for a man-to-man talk. They talked of Joe's duties as man of the house, and how Uncle Simon wanted both Grandmother and Joe to come live with him as soon as he could arrange it.

Then Uncle Simon walked Joe a little farther away so they could be absolutely alone. "Your friend Peter—" began Uncle Simon.

"He's not a close friend," said Joe. "I don't know him that well. He is one of the friendliest disciples. And the noisiest. He's big and brave and strong. I just meant that I wish I'd been there too. I would have stuck up for Jesus the same as he did."

"That's what I wanted to tell you," said Uncle Simon. "He didn't."

"He didn't? He didn't what?"

"He didn't 'stick up' for Jesus, as you say."

"What do you mean?" Joe's face was anxious. "You said he didn't run away in the garden. You said he followed Jesus."

"Yes, that's true. And I'm sure he meant to stick by Jesus just the same as you said *you* would. But when the time came—" Uncle Simon took Joe by the shoulders and looked him straight in the eyes—"when the time came, Joe—he didn't. They asked him out in the courtyard—the soldiers and the servants asked him—if he was one of the disciples. And he said no."

Joe winced as if he had been struck.

"And they asked him again, a little later, and he said no. And they asked him a third time. And he cursed and swore. He said he was not one of Jesus' disciples—that He didn't even *know* Jesus. 'I never knew the man!' he said."

Joe stared down at his feet for a moment. And then he kicked at a stone fiercely. It hurt his toe and he yelped in pain and anger. "I wouldn't have done that!" he said. He meant it to sound fierce, but it came out like a sob.

Oh, rats. He was going to cry. He hated himself.

"You don't know for sure, Joe," Uncle Simon said quietly. "You haven't been put to the test. You just don't know what you would have done."

Joe's nose was beginning to run.

Uncle Simon cleared his throat. And then, "I might have said I didn't know Him, too," he said sadly. "Or I might have run away too, up in the garden."

"*You*, Uncle Simon?"

"I just don't know," said Uncle Simon. "We can all be very brave when we're just *talking*."

Joe swallowed hard. "Where is He now? Is He on trial now?"

"Well, the whole council—the complete Supreme Court—couldn't try Him until this morning. So they're probably started by now." And then he looked up at the sky and said quickly, "We've got to get started. Joe, take care of your grandmother."

"Yes, Uncle Simon."

"And take care of Molly." Uncle Simon squeezed Joe's shoulder and started back toward the others.

"They can't possibly do anything to Him," Grandmother was saying as they drew near. "They can't do anything to Him," she said again, turning to Uncle Simon. "Can they?"

"I don't *think* so," he said.

"Is there a chance that they *can* do something then? What do they have against Him? What are they accusing Him of?"

"Well it all boils down to one thing," said Uncle Simon, checking the ropes around the donkey to make sure the bundles would be firm. "They kept asking Him if He was claiming to be the Messiah—the Son of God."

"And?"

"And He said He was."

"He actually said He was the Messiah?"

"Yes, He did."

"Well!" they said. And then they were silent again, thinking of this. Unbelievable!

And then they were suddenly leaving. Two of the children were hiked up on the donkey. Uncle Simon swept the smallest one up in his strong arms. Aunt Rachel walked alongside, a huge bundle of tied-up clothing on her head. There was much laughter and calling out last good-byes and promises to get together soon again. And finally they were gone.

Grandmother and Joe stood looking at each other, and Grandmother saw the pleading in Joe's eyes. "Yes, go ahead, Joseph," she said. "Go pick up Andy and go down and see what's going on. I'll clean up."

He thanked her and dashed to the street, then dashed back to say, "Get going!" to Molly, then dashed over to give Grandmother a hug—and finally was on his way, hurrying down the street.

If Jesus *was* the Messiah, then everything was going to be all right. If He was the Messiah, then they couldn't do anything to Him. Joe quickened his pace and headed for Andy's house.

And then he had a sudden vision of Temple police in the night with their torches and their swords—

And the high priests with their stern faces—

And the guards standing by—

And Peter waiting outside in the cold. Perhaps warming his icy hands at a fire. Yes, he thought, they probably had a charcoal fire.

And the terror of it struck him suddenly.[3]

He felt sorry for Peter.

And he thought about himself.

Would he have stayed and fought?

Suddenly he wasn't so sure.

3. Suddenly he saw how frightening it was.

# Chapter Eleven

# FRIDAY–LATER

Joe and Andy made their way through the twisting cobbled streets, struggling in the crowd. It was impossible to hurry. The crowd was so thick you couldn't poke holes in it and squeeze through no matter how hard you tried. The boys were lost in a jumble of people and donkeys and carts—and even an occasional camel. Joe filled Andy in on everything he knew; it turned out that Andy knew as much, for his father had come home from the morning worship and told it all at their breakfast too. Usually there was a spirit of friendly competition about this sort of thing—to see which one knew the most. But there was none of that this morning. They were very solemn as they compared notes and talked together.

When they got near the Temple area the confusion was incredible.[1] There was something different about the crowd now. The holiday spirit was gone. And the spirit of worship was gone. And the joy. This was a strange crowd; some of them were angry, but most of

1. It was so great you just couldn't believe it.

83

them were curious. Everyone was asking questions. And almost everyone seemed to have answers. And the rumors were flying so fast that it was impossible to put the pieces together.

"He was with the chief priests for hours."

"Since about three o'clock this morning, I guess."

"He said He is the Son of God. Did you hear that?"

"He said He is the Messiah."

"He stood before the whole council this morning. They met officially."[2]

"They asked Him there too. And He said He is the Messiah."

"Well they can't put Him to death for that! They have no authority."

"They're taking Him to Pilate."

"The *governor?!?*"

"Yes—to Pilate!"

"They'll try to persuade Pilate to sentence Him to death."

"How can they do that?"

"They'll think of something!"

Joe and Andy grabbed each other's hands and hung on tight, swept along with the crowd. Joe's heart was pounding now; there didn't seem to be enough air to breathe. But he kept on going. They were headed toward the Fortress of Antonia, built high on a rock cliff northwest of the Temple, its high corner towers rising into the Jerusalem sky. Pilate made his headquarters there, for there were apartments and courtyards and baths aplenty. But it was a mixture of splendor and gloom, for there were also barracks for soldiers. And cells for prisoners. For the Fortress of Antonia was used both as a palace and a prison.

If anything happened to Jesus of Nazareth—it would happen there.

As the people turned in that direction, Joe and Andy, who had been in the back of the crowd, suddenly found themselves in the front.

But they did not see Jesus. He had already been taken inside.

---

2. The chief priests and elders met during the night, sort of "off the cuff." But they could not call an official meeting of the whole council until morning.

The members of the Sanhedrin[3] were outside. But even they did not go beyond the outer court.

Joe knew why. Any little Jewish boy would. It was still Passover day; it had started at sundown the night before—and it would still be Passover day until sundown tonight. Today was the holiest day, the high spot of the entire week. And tomorrow was the Sabbath.

Phew.

No good Jew would enter a house that had unleavened bread in it![4]

He would have to remember that the Temple leaders didn't go in, he thought. He would have to remember everything, every little detail, to tell Grandmother when he got home.

And then he realized that the crowd was suddenly becoming quiet. Everyone was shushing everyone else.

Pilate was coming out into the court from the judgment hall!

Pilate—the governor himself!

Joe and Andy stood in awe, their mouths hanging open. Everyone was quiet now.

"What is your charge against this man?" Pilate said to the leaders. "What are you accusing Him of?"

"He's a criminal! We wouldn't have brought Him to you if He wasn't a criminal!" they said. Then they all began to shout at once.

*Criminal!*

Joe's stomach was in knots.

"What'll he do?" Joe said to Andy.

"I don't know," Andy said. "Pilate's going back inside again."

Joe and Andy used the time to get themselves a spot where they could see better. They found a ledge and climbed up on it. Ah, now, that was better. Now they could see very well. Pilate was coming out. And the crowd became quiet again.

"He says He is a king!" Pilate said, "but His kingdom is not of this world. He is not a criminal. He's not guilty of any crime."

The hubbub began again.

3. The Jewish Supreme Court.
4. Bread made without yeast.

"But He's causing riots!"

"He's against the government!"

"He talks against the government wherever He goes. Yes—from Galilee to Jerusalem!"

Pilate held up his hands for them to stop. "Is He from Galilee then?" he said. And he turned to his officers and gave some orders.

"What's he going to do?" Nobody actually said it, but the question just seemed to hang in the air, and the crowd strained forward until the answer was passed back, person to person.

"He's going to send Him to Herod."

*"King* Herod?"

"Yes, if He's from Galilee, He's under Herod's jurisdiction."[5]

Pilate disappeared inside again, his officers with him. A few soldiers remained outside, on guard.

"I don't think they're going to do anything to Him, Andy," Joe said. "You heard the governor say He wasn't guilty."

"It's a frame-up," said a man, just ahead of them, "and the governor knows it."

The next hour was one of indecision for Joe and Andy. What to do? Jesus of Nazareth had been taken away under heavy guard. Would He come back? Would the governor come back out? They couldn't decide whether to stay on the ledge where they could see, or to fight their way over to Herod's palace. They decided to sit down on the ledge where they had been standing, and sweat it out. To Joe it seemed like the longest wait of his life. They sat there silent; they had nothing more to say to each other. There was nothing to do but wait. The cool of the morning had gone now; the sun was beating down.

Then, *finally*—

Pilate came out again.

And again the crowd got quiet.

"I have examined this man thoroughly," he said. "And I find Him innocent. King Herod came to the same conclusion, and he sent

5. King Herod was ruler over that territory. And he was in Jerusalem during Passover week, the same as Pilate was.

Him back to us. nothing this man has done calls for the death penalty. Therefore—"

The crowd waited, holding its breath.

"Therefore, as you know, it's the governor's custom to release one Jewish prisoner each year during the Passover celebration. Which I shall do now."

The crowd was quiet, quiet.

"You may have your choice. I will release to you either Barabbas—"

*Barabbas!*

He was wanted for murder. He was public enemy number one. He was the most notorious[6] criminal in all the land! Everyone had heard of Barabbas.

Joe's heart leaped in sudden wild hope.

"Barabbas—or—" said Pilate.

It was absolutely still, everywhere.

"—Or Jesus of Nazareth, your Messiah!"

And then, way down in front, they began to shout. Joe couldn't believe his ears.

"Barabbas!!!"

And the crowd picked up the shout.

"Barabbas!!!"

"Release to us Barabbas!"

"Then what shall I do with Jesus, your Messiah?" said Pilate.

Again, down in front. "Crucify Him!"

"Why?" said Pilate. "What has He done wrong?"

But down in front they kept shouting.

"Crucify Him!"

And others picked it up. And the word spread across the crowd like a brush fire.

"Crucify! Crucify!"

And it became a mighty roar, as they began to chant, shouting, "Kill Him! Kill Him! Kill Him!"

Pilate held up his hands for silence. It took longer for the crowd

6. He was famous for a lot of things and they were all *bad!*

to get quiet now. A strange and wild excitement had gotten hold of them.

"Why?!?" Now Pilate had to shout. "What crime has He committed? I find no reason to sentence Him to death!" Quickly he barked some orders to his soldiers. And then back to the crowd. "I will have Him whipped, and let Him go!" He turned to his soldiers and they disappeared inside. Then Pilate swirled around and went inside too, his robes billowing out behind him like a wind-filled sail.

Joe was nearly sobbing now with relief. A whipping was bad enough. But at least they'd let Him go, and He'd be alive. Pilate himself had said he'd let Him go! Joe and Andy tried to talk, but they couldn't hear themselves. People were shouting at each other, and nobody was really listening.

Joe thought he could not bear any more. His feet hurt from balancing himself on the ledge. And his head hurt. He hurt all over. And he was thirsty. He began to wonder what time it was, and if he should be getting back to Grandmother. It would be a losing fight, trying to get through the crowd.

And then something shocked him back to attention

"They're bringing Him out, they're bringing Him out."

"There He is!"

Joe sagged with shock. Nothing in all his life had ever prepared him for this. Jesus of Nazareth was between two soldiers.

And on His head was a crown made of thorns.

They had put a royal robe on Him too.

A red robe.

And He had been beaten beyond belief.

With a whip, yes—but that was not all.

They had bashed His face with their fists.

They had pulled chunks out of His beard.

They had spit upon Him.

Joe stuck his knuckles in his mouth and bit down on them, hard, to keep from crying out.

The Jewish officials down in front cried out again, "Crucify!"

"I find Him not guilty!" Pilate bellowed in impatience.

"If you release this man you are no friend of Caesar's," they bellowed back.

Ah, that was a threat.

Pilate had once used the money from the Temple treasury to build a water supply. That was a no-no. And he had once marched his soldiers into Jerusalem by night, bearing *his* image on their standards.[7] And *that* was a no-no.

He had done all this. And more.

They were threatening to report him to Rome!

Phew.

"Crucify!" they shouted again.

"What? Crucify your King?"

"We have no king but Caesar!" The crowd had gone absolutely mad now.

"Kill Him! KILL HIM!"

It was no longer a crowd.

It was a mob now.

It was rabble.

The din reached the sky.

Joe saw it through a haze of tears.

Pilate gave some orders to his officers.

In a moment some servants brought back a bowl of water.

And then he washed his hands before them all.

What would he do, Joe thought desperately, what would he do? What would he say?

Joe leaned over from his ledge and tugged at the shoulder of a man pressed up against it. "What does it mean, his washing his hands? What does it mean? What will he do? I can't hear!"

"He's washing his hands of the whole affair," the man said.

"Does that mean he'll have Jesus killed?" Joe shouted in the man's ear.

"It means he'll carry out the execution all right. But he washes his hands to show that it wasn't *his* idea. He thinks the man is innocent."

---

7. Their law said *no graven images* in their holy city!

The last thing Joe saw before he clambered down from the ledge was the soldiers leading Jesus of Nazareth back into the palace again.

"Where are they taking Him now?" he asked the man.

"Probably back to the barracks," the man said.

Joe wiggled off the ledge, Andy behind him.

---

Joe never knew how he got home. He and Andy had struggled through the crowds without saying a word, neither of them daring to speak. What they had seen was too awful; they were shocked into silence. They parted at Andy's corner without speaking, and Joe went the rest of the way alone. He was sick in his stomach now, his breath coming in little gasps.

When Grandmother saw him coming in the door, she stopped in her tracks, shocked.

"Joseph?" she said in alarm. "Joseph!"

And then he ran into her arms.

And the tears came.

She stood there holding him, rocking gently back and forth.

It had been a long, long time since he had cried.

And it had been a long time since he and Grandmother had hugged each other like this.

He was drenched with sweat, and his clothes were stuck to him. And his hair was wet on his forehead and on his neck.

He thought he screamed it.

He meant to scream it.

But when it came out, it came out in a little shaky whisper.

"Grandmother—my friend? Jesus of Nazareth?"

"Yes—yes?"

"They're going to kill Him."

Chapter Twelve

# FRIDAY-
# STILL
# LATER

Grandmother and Joe fought their way through downtown Jerusalem. She had thrown a shawl over her head, and in her haste had forgotten to take off her apron. It was still tucked around her hips.

The crowds were greater than ever now, if that were possible, for it was now about nine o'clock in the morning and more people were up. The word had spread like wildfire to every corner of Jerusalem, and everyone who could possibly walk was out to see what it was all about.

A crucifixion!

And on Passover day!

Grandmother was good at poking her way through the crowds and making holes for her and Joe to squeeze through. She was better than good; she was fantastic. Much better than Andy and almost as good as Uncle Simon. Her bony body could squeeze through the tiniest places, and in her zeal[1] she seemed to have the strength of ten men.

1. That's gung-ho gusto, in this case.

Joe followed her in surprise, and sometimes, the way she pushed herself through—in alarm. If she wasn't more careful she would get them both in trouble. She would dart ahead and be gone, and then he would hurry and catch up with her. Sometimes he thought he wasn't going to make it. And he wondered whether Grandmother was taking care of him or he was taking care of Grandmother.

It was true.

She was merry,

She was gentle,

She was a tiger,

And sometimes she was IMPOSSIBLE.

This was one of those times.

She was darting ahead now, squeezing sideways, close to the shops, looking for a hole. Then she found one, and disappeared. Joe plunged through after her. Then she stopped suddenly. He nearly climbed up her back. They were right in front now, in the crowd that was lining the street. They listened, piecing together what had happened since Joe had left.

"There are three of them, you know."

"Three?"

"Yes. They're crucifying two others with Him."

"And what did they do?"

"Oh, just a couple of thieves. You'll see when they come by. It'll be printed on their signs."[2]

"And what did they print on His sign?"

"Pilate printed it himself. 'Jesus of Nazareth, King of the Jews.' It's written in three languages—Hebrew and Greek and Latin."

"But that's no crime."

"Crime or no crime—that's what it says."

And then the word was passed along that they were drawing near. And everyone strained forward to see.

The gossip was right. There were three of them. With four soldiers around each one, prodding them on. The procession was slow, very

2. The crime was always printed on a sign to be carried ahead of the criminal and tacked up later on his cross, so that people could see what he had done.

93

slow. The three prisoners staggered along. The streets were cobbled and winding, up steps and down steps and around curves; the going was hard. And the crosses were heavy.

"Hold it! Hooooold it—"

There were steps up ahead. And the whole procession lumbered to a halt, with one of the prisoners right in front of Joe and Grandmother. The end of His cross bumped to a stop on the cobblestones. And Joe looked up at the Man under the weight of it. His face had been so badly beaten that He could have been anybody. But His eyes, with all the sadness of the world in them, burned through, straight at Joe.

And Joe knew that he was looking into the eyes of Jesus of Nazareth.

And the world seemed to stand still.

"Joseph."

Had he really heard it or had he imagined it?

"Joseph Simon Bar-Jason."

Someone had spoken his name.

He had not taken his eyes off the face of Jesus of Nazareth, and Jesus' lips had not moved. But Joe knew, as sure as he was standing there, that Jesus had called him by name.

He knows me, he thought, He *does* know me—He knows all about me—my name, and everything I ever did and everything I ever thought.

And a feeling of wonder and joy shot through Joe and his heart pounded. He wanted to cry out, but no sound came. Something wonderful and mysterious had happened to him; he would never be the same again.

And in all his life he would never find the words to tell about how he felt at that moment.

Even when he was a very old man, and very wise.

He could tell what *happened.*

But he would never be able to tell *how he felt* when the world stood still this day.

And then the procession began to move again. And Jesus of Nazareth tightened His grip on His cross and struggled on. The

94

third prisoner followed, and the soldiers; then the crowd poured into the street and closed behind them and they were out of sight. Joe was pushed forward and nearly fell headlong.

He and Grandmother trudged along as best they could. Grandmother squeezing ahead again, somehow always finding a place to get through.

And then, once again the procession stopped suddenly, the people bumping heads and climbing up backs. This time it wasn't a bend in the streets, or it wasn't steps. This time Jesus of Nazareth had staggered with exhaustion under the weight of the cross, and the Roman soldiers had ordered a passing man to help him carry it. Joe and Grandmother got the news as it filtered back. Joe and Grandmother strained to listen, to find out what happened.

"Who was the man?"

"I don't know—somebody from Africa. Just come into town for Passover week. Fellow by the name of Simon. He's from Cyrene."

Joe pictured Simon, tall and dark-skinned and strong, standing behind Jesus and hiking the heavy end of the cross upon his own shoulder. He wished fiercely that he were tall and strong, that he could have been up there to help.

The crowd moved on and poured out of the city gate, all of them—the Roman soldiers and the Temple leaders and Jesus and the two thieves and the people, as if Jerusalem had spewed them out.

And then Joe realized where they were going. They were headed to a low rocky hill, just north of the city, near a highway. It was a hill called "The Skull." He'd been up there on hikes with Andy many times. If you backed off far enough away and looked at it, it *looked* like a skull.

By the time Joe and Grandmother caught up, the Crucifixion had already begun. They had laid the cross on the ground and laid Him on it. And they had bound His upper arms with ropes to the crossbeam, and nailed His hands to it. And they'd nailed His feet to the bottom of the upright. And they'd set the cross in the hole that had been dug for it. He was between the two thieves. And nailed up over His head was the sign: JESUS OF NAZARETH, KING OF THE JEWS.

"The Temple leaders wanted Pilate to change that," a man nearby muttered to his neighbor.

"Change it to what?"

"Well they wanted him to write HE *SAID* I AM KING OF THE JEWS."

"Pilate wouldn't do it?"

"No. Pilate wouldn't do it. He said that's what he had written and that's the way it was going to stay—exactly as it was."

The crowd grew thicker as the people kept pouring out from the city. Some of them managed to scramble up and find a spot on the hill; others watched from the road below. It was as if a madness had seized them, even more terrible than before. They hurled insults at Him, trying to outshout each other. Much of it was lost in the din. Some of it could be heard loud and clear, from the hill down to the highway.

"Come on down from the cross if You're the Son of God!"

"He saved others, but He can't save Himself!"

"Come down from the cross and we'll believe You!"

"Didn't He say, 'I am the Son of God'?"

"Didn't He say He is the Messiah?"

"Ha!"

Joe squinched his fists at his sides. Why doesn't He save Himself, he thought, why doesn't He? If He is the Messiah, why doesn't He?

And then—

The crowd grew quiet as if some great voice had said "Stop!"

And right in the midst of a blazing sunny day—

It suddenly got dark. It was a strange, eerie[3] darkness. Not just the darkness of a storm. It was something different. Something like they had never seen before. People huddled together, shivering.

And the sneers stopped,

And the insults,

And the jeering,

All stopped, just stopped.

3. **Spooky.**

And people were filled with a nameless fear.

*What was going to happen?*

But the moments ticked away, and nothing did happen. So they began to murmur among themselves softly, and watch. And wait. And wonder.

Joe and Grandmother stood close, close, her arm around his shoulder. They didn't say a word. They had no idea how long they stood that way. They had no idea how much time had gone by.

Then, suddenly—

They heard a shout.

Different from all the other shouting.

It rang out through the air— "It is FINISHED!"

It was a cry of triumph! A cry of victory!

And the One who had shouted—was Jesus of Nazareth.

Joe began to tremble.

Everyone waited, breathless.

And then Jesus shouted again. "Father, into Your hands I place My spirit!"

Joe stood there stunned. It was the prayer he prayed at night, kneeling beside Grandmother.

The words seemed to hang in the air, ringing.

No one moved.

Jesus had *said* that no man could take His life from Him—that He would *lay it down Himself* when the time came.

Is this what He had just done?

Joe looked up toward Grandmother to ask her what she thought it meant. But he never got the words out. For at that moment, everything began to happen at once.

The earth began to tremble and shake.

The rocks broke—just split down the middle.

And the crowd began to break up, crumbling off at the edges like one of Grandmother's biscuits. And then it seemed to crack and fall apart, as everybody began to scatter in all directions—some beating their breasts, some tearing their clothing, many of them crying out in fear and wonder.

Then Joe was jostled by somebody running past. Actually he was more than jostled: he was spun around and nearly knocked off his feet. Then Grandmother tugged at his sleeve. And they turned, her arm around his shoulder, and followed the crowd.

It was hard going back down the hill. They slipped and stumbled and sent stones scurrying before them. They went back down the road, and back through the gate into the city. There they got caught in a huge traffic jam that had developed around the Temple area. And there the rumors were flying—people reporting to each other what they had seen and what they had heard.

"The curtain in the Temple has been torn!"

"What curtain?" Joe asked Grandmother. But she shushed him and they listened.

"The curtain that covers the Holy place!" someone answered back. What? The holiest place in the Temple?

"It's been torn from the top down, as if giant unseen hands had torn it in two!"

"You can't mean that!"

"Yes! They say it's true! It happened at the same moment the earth began to tremble."

Joe stubbed his toe on a stone step, and he and Grandmother scrambled up toward the street that would lead them home. The holy curtain torn! That was the same moment Jesus had said, "Father, into Your hands I place My spirit," Joe thought. That was the moment He had laid down His life of His own accord! Why did the two things happen at once? What did it mean? And why did the earth tremble?

He kept following Grandmother, his questions unanswered. They had both decided to head for home, without saying so. It was as though they were both just too tired to talk about it. Joe's very bones hurt. They walked the rest of the way without saying a word.

Molly was fussing and clucking when they got in the yard. She protected her eggs with threats of violence, and scolded Joe angrily when he got near. "You'd think she was protecting a walled city," Joe grumbled to Grandmother. And he was surprised to find himself talking about ordinary things again. How could he talk about Molly?

What difference did Molly make now? Jesus of Nazareth wasn't the Messiah after all. He was gone. They'd killed Him.

They would take Him down before sunset.

Joe wondered who would do it.

Would the Roman soldiers do it?

And where would they put Him?

Grandmother was heating water for their baths, and getting their evening meal ready. For in a short time it would be sundown, and the Sabbath would begin. And a very special Sabbath at that. It was *the* Sabbath of Passover week. And right now, the day that was ending was *the* special preparation day for the Passover week Sabbath.

And what a strange day it had been.

Joe did his evening chores. He and Grandmother went through the motions of finishing up the day.

But Grandmother dragged her feet.

And Joe felt as if somebody had let the air out of him.

And then it came. He heard the evening psalm from the Temple.

"The Lord reigneth . . ."

And he knew that they were slaying the lamb at the Temple. How could they go on like this, he thought, as if nothing had happened?

Molly took her evening walk, and then cooed and fussed and got her brood-to-be to bed.

"You're dragging your feet, Molly," Joe laughed. And she squawked back at him.

But after he was in his own bed and it was dark, his nose began to run.

And his throat ached.

And he turned his face to the wall.

And he realized that he was crying.

# Chapter Thirteen

# SATURDAY (SABBATH)

It was the morning of the Sabbath.
The day you couldn't sew two stitches,
Or tie a knot—unless it could be untied with one hand.
You couldn't write letters,
Or sock anything with a hammer,
Or carry anything from one property to another,
Or sow seed,
Or plow,
Or thresh grain or grind it,
Or shear wool or wash it or beat it,
Or spin it,
Or *spit*.

You couldn't travel more than two miles. But you could travel almost anywhere in your mind, and nobody could say a word about it.

Joe and Grandmother had been to early morning worship. They had stayed in the outer court listening to the music—

"It is a good thing to give thanks unto the Lord . . ."

And though they couldn't see it, they knew the lamb had been slain.

After the service, Grandmother had gossiped with some of the women, and Joe had stood by and listened hard. Yes, they had taken Jesus of Nazareth down from the cross before sunset, before the Sabbath began last evening.[1]

"And who took Him down," Grandmother asked, "the Roman soldiers?"

And everybody began to tell her at once.

"No. Two members of the Jewish Sanhedrin."

"The leaders of the Temple?" Grandmother almost shouted. And Joe picked up his ears.

"Yes. They were secret followers of Jesus. Have been all along. Afraid to come out with it—afraid they'd get clobbered by the rest of the council."

"One of them was a man named Joseph—from Arimathea. (Air-ah-mah-*theé*-ah)[2]

"He went to Pilate and asked him if he could have charge of the body of Jesus—"[3]

"And Nicodemus (Nick-oh-*deé*-mus). Another member of the council."

"They went away together. With spices. And they wrapped Him in a linen cloth and took Him away."

"To a tomb!"

"They did it quickly, before sundown—before Sabbath began."

"Where?" Joe tugged at Grandmother's sleeve and whispered it. He was too polite to speak out to the other grown-ups. But he had to know.

"Hush, Joseph," Grandmother said. "Just listen."

1. It was not lawful for a Jew to touch a dead body on the Sabbath, so it had to be done quickly.
2. It was a town not far from Jerusalem, to the northwest.
3. He asked for permission to take Him down from the cross and to take charge of the burial.

"Joseph of Arimathea owned some property right nearby," one of them said, "with a new tomb. They put Him there."

"Anyone else around?" said Grandmother.

"A few. A man. Some women. Some said they were His closest friends. But I don't know who they were."

But where, thought Joe, *where?*

"Such a business!" one of them said, changing the subject. "In all my life I can't remember such a Passover as this one. It's a Passover to end all Passovers, you might say."

"Yes—there hasn't been so much excitement since the very first Passover when the Jews left Egypt," said another.

And then they grew suddenly quiet, as if they were afraid they had trampled on something very solemn. Whatever had happened was a great mystery; none of them could fathom[4] it. And they giggled nervously because secretly they were a little afraid of it. There was something in the air—a fear, a gloom. It was almost as if the sky were dark again. It was almost as if they did not dare talk about it anymore.

Joe felt it too. He couldn't seem to shake it off.

Joe and Grandmother headed for home after that. They had their noonday meal, and again Joe missed Grandmother's delicious biscuits. In a way he'd be almost glad when Passover was over.

Then Grandmother decided to take a nap; she was still exhausted from yesterday. Joe asked her if he could pick up Andy and if they could wander around a bit. She said yes, and reminded him of all the things he *couldn't* do. He couldn't tie a knot or walk more than two miles or carry anything from one property to another—

"Or shoot a deer," teased Joe. And they both chuckled, for they knew he didn't have a weapon, not even a sling.

"And I won't spit," said Joe, calling over his shoulder as he went out the door.

"Bite your tongue, Joe!" she called back after him.

He laughed again, and stooped to look at Molly's eggs. She had gone around the side of the house for her daily exercise.

---

4. None of them could dig deep enough to figure it out.

Was that a tiny hole in one of them?

*Was that a hole?*

He brushed it with his fingers, carefully.

No—he guessed it wasn't. It was just a mark on the egg.

"Molly ole boy," he said, as she came back around the corner, "I thought for a minute you were really getting somewhere. But now I'm beginning to think you're a phony. You've been fooling us all, all this time. There's nothing in those eggs."

She looked at him sorrowfully.

"They're hollow!" he said as he went out into the street. And he laughed again.

When he got out on the street alone, though, the gloom inside him was so deep, he felt he could not bear it. He had a deep desire now to check out all the facts, to try to solve the mystery. Where had they buried Jesus of Nazareth anyhow?

As soon as he picked up Andy, they started their trek around the downtown section of Jerusalem. They walked through the crooked streets, up steps and down steps, and past the quiet shops.

It was Sabbath.

The shops were closed.

There was no business,

And no washings blowing on the rooftops,

And no loud haggling over the purchase of groceries,

And no loud talking by tourists shopping for souvenirs to take home.

They went past the house of Caiaphas, the high priest. Everything was quiet there; the court was empty. They looked up at the forbidding Fortress of Antonia. Except for guards outside, and soldiers coming and going, there was nothing doing there either. Joe wondered where Pilate was.

And he wondered how Pilate felt.

Then they headed out the gate, and up toward Skull Hill.

The crosses were gone. There was no evidence of yesterday's horror. The ground was trampled and scuffed; you could tell that a mob had been there, that was all.

"Did you know that one of the thieves asked Jesus to forgive him?" asked Andy.

"No," said Joe. "How do you know this?"

"My father was up near the front," said Andy. "And so was my uncle. I was in back with my mother and aunt. But they all talked about it, far into the night. I lay on my bed and listened. I was in bed, but I could hear."

"What else, what else?" said Joe.

"Well from the cross, Jesus said, 'Father, forgive these people; they don't know what they're doing!'"

"And what about the thieves," Joe said. "Did He forgive them?"

"No," said Andy. "Not both of them. One of them."

Joe waited, listening, his mouth open.

"The other one cursed and swore at Him. And mocked Him. He said, 'So You're the Messiah, are You? Well prove it by saving Yourself—and us too, while You're at it!' But the other thief said that they deserved to die for their evil deeds. But that Jesus hadn't done anything wrong. And then he asked Jesus to remember him when He came into His kingdom."

"He said *that?*" said Joe, "when He came into His *kingdom?!?*"

"Yes He did."

"Then he *did* believe that Jesus was the Messiah."

"Yes. I guess he must have believed that."

"What did Jesus say?" Joe's voice had gone up a few notches, in excitement.

"He made a solemn promise," said Andy. "That was what He called it. A solemn promise. He said—'Today you will be with Me—*in Paradise.*'"

"Pheeeeeewwwwww." Joe let his breath out slowly. "And he believed that Jesus *was* the Messiah," he said again.

"The captain of the Roman soldiers who were handling the execution believed it too. But not until after Jesus was dead."

"What do you mean?" said Joe.

"Just that after Jesus was dead, the Roman captain cried out, 'Surely this was the Son of God.' He said that when the earth began to shake. Were you there when the earth began to shake?"

"Yes, yes," Joe said impatiently. "Was there anything else? Can you think of anything else?"

"I can't remember anything else," Andy said. "Here. Down this way."

They scrambled down the other side of the hill, and then up the road again, and then up a path. Andy went ahead, parting brush as they went along, and Joe followed, sweating now—partly from the heat. But mostly from excitement. He remembered now. He and Andy had hiked up this way once. He remembered the path. And he remembered the entrance to the garden. It had been a private garden and they had not gone beyond the entrance. "I remember this place," he began, "we hiked—"

Andy suddenly stopped in front, and put his hand up for silence.

They were not alone.

There were voices up ahead.

Low, mumbling.

Coming from the garden.

Joe and Andy sneaked up to the entrance.

And stopped.

And listened.

"They're soldiers," Joe whispered. But Andy shushed him, his finger to his lips.

They *were* soldiers. They were the Temple police!

And there was the tomb. And there was the huge circular stone door. It was shaped like a disk and it was set in a trough so it could be rolled like a great wheel. It had been rolled, all right—right over the opening, to shut it tight.

And it was sealed—

*With Pilate's official seal!*[5]

Wow!

The boys stopped, struck dumb, and waited. Joe could smell blossoms. There were almond trees in bloom; they had burst out

---

5. The members of the Jewish Sanhedrin had gone to Pilate and asked him for an order to seal the tomb until the third day, so Jesus' disciples could not come and steal the body.

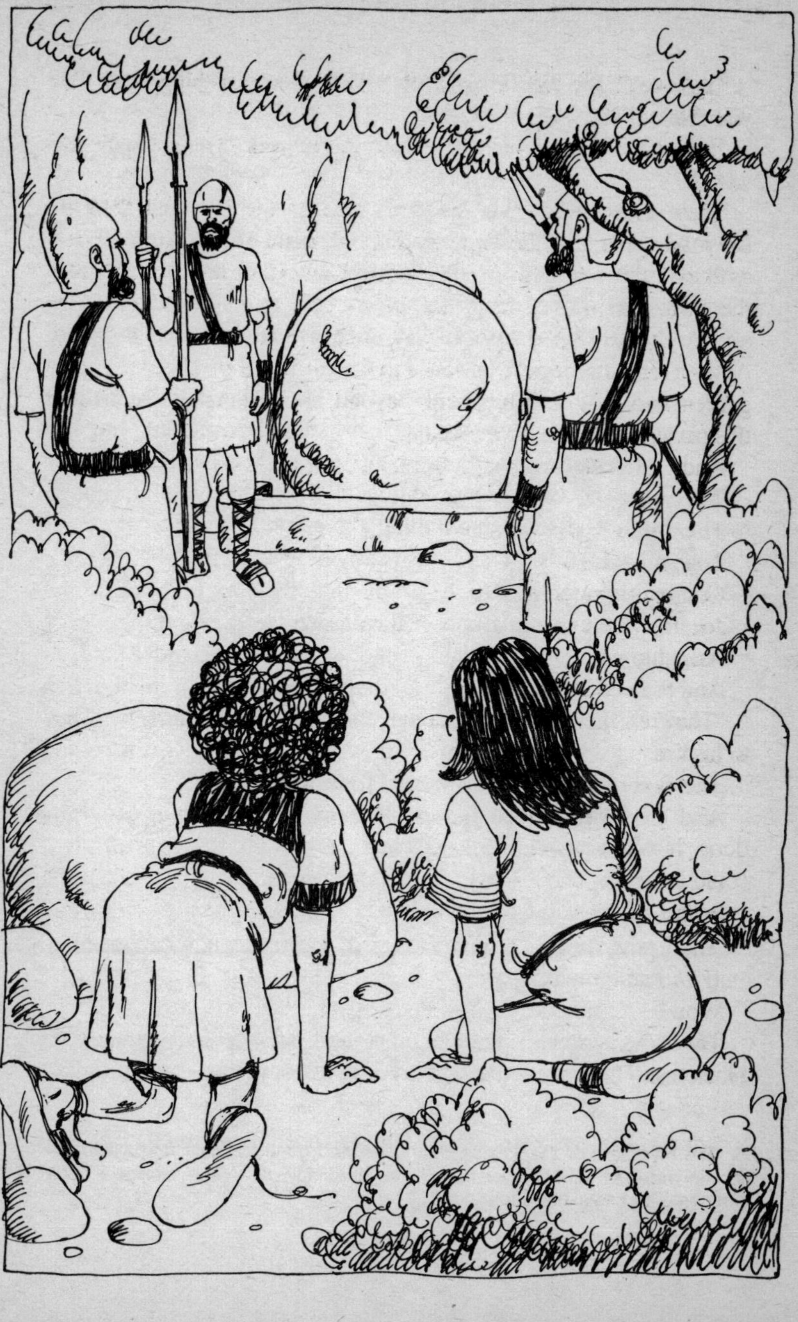

early after the spring rains. And windflowers were sweeping like mad over everything, poking up between the rocks and climbing the hill on the other side.

He remembered what Jesus had said about the windflowers. "Lilies of the field" He had called them. "Look at the lilies," He had said. "Solomon in all his glory was not robed as well as they are. If God provides clothing for the flowers, don't you suppose He will provide for you?"

Joe looked at the tomb, silent and fearsome. After all Jesus had said, why didn't He save Himself?

Joe swallowed a lump in his throat. He signaled to Andy that he wanted to leave. Andy shrugged his shoulders, turned, and followed him back down the path.

"There was no use staying," Joe said when they got far enough away to talk. "There wasn't anything to see."

"Right," said Andy. "There wasn't anything to see."

Neither of them wanted to admit that they were afraid of the soldiers. And they were afraid of the garden too. Beyond the silence was another greater silence that neither of them could understand.

They walked back the same way they came, neither of them saying a word until they got back through the gate and into the city. They looked at the sky and the long shadows on the streets. It was getting late. So without a word they headed for home.

After a long time Joe found his tongue. "Do you suppose any of His disciples have been there?"

"Where?"

"At the tomb."

"No," said Andy. "I haven't heard. I know what happened to one of them though."

"You do?" said Joe. "Was it Peter?"

"Nope. It was the other one. The one we saw walking with his head down."

"Judas?"

"Judas. That was the one." They were at his corner now, and he turned up his street.

"What did you hear?" said Joe.

108

"He's dead," said Andy. "He hanged himself." And he broke into a run.

_____

That night Joe lay on his mat and listened to Grandmother snoring softly. He had come home and told her all that had happened, all that he'd been able to find out from Andy.

She was a good listener.

Her eyes would squint,

And then grow round,

And squint again.

Then she'd lean forward to catch what was coming next.

Telling Grandmother something was like living it all over again. The way she listened, it came back to life. Joe had finished his story dramatically.

"And Judas hanged himself."

"He *what?*"

"He hanged himself, Grandmother. That's what they said."

She'd looked back at him round-eyed without saying a word. A great gloom had settled over them and over the whole house.

And then there had been the song from the Temple—

"It's a good thing to give thanks unto the Lord . . ."

—and the Sabbath was over. They'd eaten their evening meal in silence. There'd been nothing left to say.

And now it was all over.

Joe lay there staring at the ceiling. The woman down at the Temple had said it lightly, but it was true, Joe thought. This did seem like the Passover to end all Passovers. There had never been anything like it before.

He thought of the psalm again that had closed the Sabbath—

"It's a good thing to give thanks unto the Lord . . ."

"Thanks for what?" he muttered under his breath. And then he

109

felt ashamed and a little frightened that such a thing had even entered his mind.

He turned over on his side,
And punched his fist into his mat.
It seemed as if God Himself were dead.

The gloom that had settled over the house, settled down in his heart, as he went to sleep.

# Chapter Fourteen

# SATURDAY NIGHT/ SUNDAY MORNING

One by one the lights went out all over Jerusalem.
In the houses,
And Herod's palace,
And the Fortress of Antonia, except for some dim lights in the barracks.

The great Temple stood white and ghostly in the night, its gold and marble gleaming only faintly in the pale moonlight. There were wispy clouds drawn over the moon like a gauzy curtain, letting only a little light through.

And deep shadows on the earth, everywhere.

There was no one stirring except for the guards on duty at the lookout posts and at the gates. Skull Hill was dark and empty, as if the great drama that had taken place there yesterday, had never been.

The garden was dark too. The windflowers had folded up for the night and the almond blossoms were quiet. And the great acacia and olive trees that towered overhead, were quiet too.

Not a leaf rustled.
Not a bird stirred.

111

The night watch was on duty, some of the soldiers lounging and talking softly, a couple of them snoozing. The small torch that they had stuck in the ground was the only light. Its flame burned straight up, smooth and glowing in the quiet air.

A great and mysterious quiet had settled down over the whole city, as if all nature was waiting for something to happen.

It was quiet, quiet.

Then SUDDENLY—

All heaven seemed to break loose!

The earth began to tremble—

The soldiers staggered to their feet—

And then—

In the twinkling of an eye—

An angel of the Lord came down!

With the speed of sound, he came, and he seemed to split the sky!

His face shone like lightning—

And his clothing was a brilliant white—

And he rolled aside that enormous stone that closed the tomb—

AND SAT ON IT!?????!!!!!!

The soldiers backed away, shaking with fear. And the angel looked at them, and—

ZAP!

They fell down in a dead faint under the awful[1] power of God.

And then all was silent once more.

And then the flame from the torch, that had been burning up straight, skittered backward.

Had someone walked past it?

There was a sense of power in the air. The birds in their nests raised their heads quickly to watch. The black of the night turned to gray. The soldiers stirred, helped each other up, and pulled their torch out of the ground and staggered away in terror.

And then it was quiet.

When the next sound came, it was very ordinary and human—the

---

1. Filled with awe, so great, there are no words to describe it.

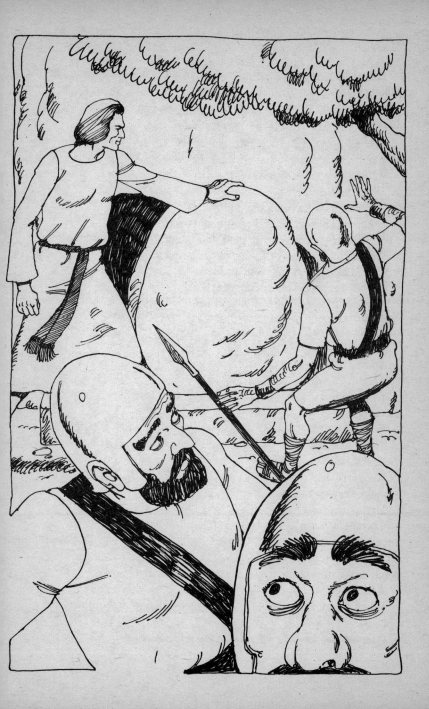

sound of women talking low. It was Mary, the mother of James. And Salome, the mother of two of His disciples.[2] And Mary Magdalene, whom He had healed a long time before. They were coming with embalming spices to prepare Jesus for a proper burial. And they were talking in low, worried tones. However would they roll aside the huge stone that covered the entrance. When they reached the garden—they stopped short.

The soldiers were gone.

The birds were beginning to stir.

The windflowers were beginning to open.

It was cool and wet with dew, and fragrant with almond blossoms. The first gray streaks of dawn had started to stretch across the sky. And in its light, they looked and saw—

The stone had been rolled away!

The entrance to the tomb was open!

2. James and John.

114

# Chapter Fifteen

# SUNDAY MORNING

Joe stirred in his sleep and squiggled further into his blanket, winding himself into a ball. It was cool. The gray light of early dawn was coming in the windows and making paths across the floor, toward his bed.

A few minutes later he unwound himself and rolled over on his back, his eyes open. Grandmother was up already, talking very softly to somebody outside. Then her voice died away as she went around the side of the house to get thorns from the thornpile for her morning fire. Then she was inside again, and he heard the clatter as she juggled her clay pots carefully, trying not to make a noise.

And then he sat bolt upright in bed.

Molly was squawking. And it was like no squawk she had ever squawked before.

Aaaaaaawh-puk-puk-puk-PUK!

It was a cry of triumph! It was a cry of VICTORY!

MOLLY?!!?

He sprang up, tangled up in his blanket, and was halfway across the room before he could get one foot free from it. He bolted out the door hopping on one foot dragging the blanket behind him.

"Molly ole boy!" he shrieked.

Molly was hovering over her nest. She looked up at him threateningly, with sparks in her eyes, as if she would fight with the strength of a tiger if anybody came too close.

And her eggs! They were lying there in a complete jumble, with baby chicks staggering over them—

Between them—

And under them, in all directions. Most of them were open, completely broken. Many of them were half open with chicks struggling to get out.

One of them was half open with a chick lying in it as if it were a cradle. He was stuck to it and couldn't get out. Joe watched him as he struggled for a few seconds and then rested, his head hanging over the edge, as limp as a wet noodle.

One egg had just a hole in it, and it trembled as the little fella inside pecked frantically, trying to get out. Another chick had snuggled against it, close, to keep warm.

And they were ALL wet and ugly, their feathers sticking close to their bodies. They seemed to be all heads.

"Molly ole boy!" Joe shrieked, "you made it!" He swung his arm around in the air in huge circles, as if he were winding up to pitch a ball or sling a stone. "I knew you'd make it!" he shouted again, doubling up and jumping up and down so hard his knees whacked against his chest. "Grandmother!" he shouted, "Molly is having her babies!" And then, "Grandmother," he shouted in a whisper, for she had come out and was standing right beside him.

"Joseph—not so loud!" she shushed him, but she was grinning.

"She made it, Grandmother! She made it! She's having her babies! I knew she'd make it."

"You did *not*," she said. "You'd lost all faith in her. I heard you call her a phony just the other night."

"I didn't mean it," Joe said. "She knows I didn't mean it." And he giggled in delight as he watched the chicks climb about in circles,

116

bumping into each other and tumbling away. "Can't I unstick that little one and help him out?"

"Nooooo," Grandmother said. "Molly would peck you if you did. Besides, you shouldn't help him. He needs to struggle."

"Why?"

"That's how he gets his strength. It's all a part of being born."

"Oh," Joe said. "Then I can't help the other one with only a hole in his egg. He's got a long way to go. Can't I help him just a little?"

"Oh, you can't touch him either." She watched for a few minutes longer. Then, "I'm going in and get breakfast," she said.

"I don't want any breakfast. I want to take four of them back to the shopkeeper. To pay him back for the one I stole. And I might see somebody on the way I can show them to." He followed Grandmother into the house.

"You just want to show them off," she said. "You can't take them right away."

"Why not?"

"Well they're too new. They're too weak. They have to dry off and fluff out first. And Molly will have to warm them under her wings. They're not ready to leave her yet."

"Well then I want to go down to the Temple and ask God to forgive me," he said. "And maybe get a dove. And make a sacrifice. And maybe I'll see somebody down there and I can tell 'em about the big birth. Twenty chicks!"

"Well then," said Grandmother, giving in, "we might as well go. We'll have breakfast when we come back."

Joe washed quickly and slipped into his clothes. And they hustled out the gate.

The narrow crooked streets were coming alive as they went along. The little shops seemed to yawn and stretch and spill their merchandise on the pavements—silks, baskets, pottery, groceries, and things to wear. People were making their way toward the Temple for the morning worship. The crowds were not as great as they'd been before, and Joe and Grandmother had an easy time getting through.

They hustled through the Court of the Gentiles, past the cages

117

and stalls, and mingled with the other people getting ready for the service.

And that's as far as they got.

That's where they heard it.

The women had gone to the tomb.

Mary Magdalene, and James' mother Mary, and Salome.

The stone had been rolled away.

And the tomb was empty!

Mary Magdalene had run back to tell the disciples.

The other women had looked in.

And there they saw—

Two men in shining garments! They were angels!

And as the women had stood there dumbstruck, the angels had said, "Why are you looking in a TOMB for someone Who is ALIVE? He is RISEN—just as He said He would. Don't just stand there. Go—tell His disciples!"

And the women had run in amazement and wonder.

Meanwhile Mary Magdalene had reached two of the disciples, and they had rushed to the tomb in absolute unbelief—

And looked in—

And left in bewilderment!

Where was He?

None of them knew.

But Mary Magdalene had stayed there in the garden. And after the disciples left, she had gone to the tomb to look for herself. And there inside were two white-robed angels sitting at the head and the foot of the place where Jesus had lain. And they'd actually spoken to her. And asked her why she was crying.

And that was not all.

She had turned around and seen someone she thought was the gardener. She'd asked him where they had put Jesus of Nazareth.

And He called her by name.

"Mary," He had said.

It was Jesus Himself!

Joe tugged at Grandmother's sleeve. "I don't get it," he said. "I don't get it. Who were the two disciples who came to the tomb?

118

Who were they?"

"The two disciples went in there," someone was saying, "And they found the cloth lying there, still folded just as it had been folded around His body. But He was gone. And the napkin that had been wrapped around His head. It was rolled up and lying there alongside. No *man* could have gotten out of those things without unwinding them. They were still wound—but He was gone."

"But who were the two disciples?" Joe asked again, but nobody heard him. They went right on talking.

"Jesus appeared to the other women, too," they were saying. "And He told them to go tell the disciples to go ahead into Galilee—that He would meet them there."

"Yes—what happened, what happened? What did they do?"

"They haven't done anything yet, as far as we know."

"Why?"

"They didn't believe it. They didn't believe what they had seen with their own eyes."

"Who were the two disciples?" Joe said again.

Grandmother heard him this time.

"Who were the two disciples?" she asked.

"One of them was the big one—the fisherman from Galilee. Peter," someone said.

Even as they had been talking, the priest had been sent to climb a high spot to look toward the east. And over the din of all the talking and all the bustle in the great courtyards, his voice rang through the morning air. "The morning shineth already!"

And even as he said it, the sun shot its rays up from the east, and they spread across the heavens and lighted up the gold on the Temple.

"Is the sky lit up as far as Hebron?" the captain called out.

"Yea—as far as Hebron!" the answer came back.

And then the order—always thrilling, always new.

"OPEN THE GATES OF THE TEMPLE!"

"BLOW THE TRUMPETS!"

And the blast of the trumpets was enough to uproot the hair

119

of your head. Joe quivered when he heard it, and his eardrums wobbled.

"SLAY THE LAMB!"

The sun was up bright now.

Joe and Grandmother waited to hear no more.

The words were still ringing in their ears. The tomb was empty! Jesus of Nazareth was gone!

Joe and Grandmother made their way through the Court of the Gentiles, bobbing and weaving, toward the gate. The choirs had started to sing—

"The earth is the Lord's . . ."

This time Joe was in the lead. Grandmother picked up her skirts and followed him. Together they hurried along the street, up the road, toward the garden where the tomb was. Joe led the way, for he knew where it was. It wasn't far but they were breathing fast when they got there, and Joe's heart was beating wildly. The people they'd met on the way all seemed to be headed for the Temple. So when they got there, they were alone.

The news had not spread far yet.

The morning song was still filling the air—

"The earth is the Lord's . . .
THE EARTH IS THE LORD'S . . ."

And a thrill shot through Joe.

Sure enough—the tomb was open!

The great wheel-like stone had been rolled aside.

Joe ran ahead until he was a few feet away from the entrance—

And then he stopped.

His mind was buzzing, trying to put pieces together. Grandmother had come up and stopped a few feet behind him, half turned, as if she were ready to run for her life if so much as a blade of grass moved. He had never seen her so frightened before.

"Don't you think we'd better go, Joseph?" she said nervously.

120

"Haven't you seen enough? You can see that He's gone."

"Do you believe it?" Joe said.

The sun was up bright now; the garden was speckled with it. Joe thought of the morning ritual at the Temple—

"The day shineth!"

"Does it light up the sky as far as Hebron?"

"Yea—as far as Hebron!"

And suddenly the words he'd been trying so hard to remember came back. "I am come, a light into the world that whosoever believeth on me should not live in darkness!"

*"Open the gate of the Temple!"*

*"Blow the trumpets!"*

Joe's mind skidded to a stop. And then—

*"Slay the lamb!"*

He looked up at Grandmother, shading his eyes from the sun. "Grandmother. You remember how we watched that man in the Temple? How he transferred his sin to the lamb?"

"Yes, Joe."

"And the lamb was killed in his place?"

"Yes Joe, yes."

"Grandmother—Jesus of Nazareth *was the lamb!*"

"Joseph Simon Bar-Jason!" Grandmother said, "Let's get back to the Temple. We'll buy a sacrifice. Transfer your sin to the sacrifice. And ask God to forgive you. And then let's get home."

"Don't you believe Jesus of Nazareth was the Messiah?" he said.

"Joseph," she said, trying to be patient. "We believe in *God.*"

And then the other words he'd been trying to remember came tumbling into his mind. "I remember something else," he went on stubbornly, "He who believes in Me—*believes in God who sent Me.*"

Grandmother had turned to go—but at that she stopped, turned around again.

"He *is* the sacrifice, Grandmother. He is the *lamb.* He is the Lamb of God."

She backed off a step, as if trying to get away from his words.

"Do you remember the woman in the Court of the Gentiles?"

he said. "When that woman said this was the Passover to end all Passovers?"

She nodded.

"Well I think it *is*. Jesus was the Passover lamb. He was killed on Passover day."

"He was a prophet," she said desperately.

"No! He was the lamb," said Joe. "He died on the cross just like the lamb died on the altar."

"Joseph—come!"

He turned to the empty tomb again. He didn't know whether to kneel down or to bow his head. He decided to bow his head. He was a little embarrassed about kneeling down in front of Grandmother.

"What are you doing?" she said.

"I'm going to ask Him to forgive me," he said. "I'm going to transfer my sin to Him."

She hesitated a minute, then came back slowly and stood beside him.

"What shall I call Him?" he said.

She thought a moment, then cleared her throat. "If that's the way you feel, Joe," she said, "you'd better call Him Lord."

---

Back at the Temple, the worship service was over. The people there had transferred their sins to the lamb on the altar, and left, to begin a new day.

And there by the empty tomb, Joseph Simon Bar-Jason transferred his sin to the Lamb of God, and left, to begin a new life.

There was only one thing wrong.

Grandmother didn't believe.

No, two.

Peter didn't believe either.

# Chapter Sixteen

# GOD AND A BOY NAMED JOE

"Boy, I thought he'd NEVER get out!" said Joe.

"He is the wettest stickiest little fella I ever saw," Grandmother chuckled. "And he did take his time, pecking his way out. See how little he is. I guess he's the runt."

"Can I pick him up?"

"No—don't touch him."

"But he can't stand up."

"He's just tired out, that's all. It's quite a struggle, getting born. He'll be all right. You'll see."

And he was. Within an hour he was climbing around the broken eggshells. And before another hour was up, he was dry and fluffy, snuggled under Molly's wings along with the rest of the chicks.

Joe had fixed her a little pile of straw to snuggle in until he cleaned her coop. But she had walked by it with her nose[1] in the air and had chosen a spot around the side of the house by the thorn pile. It was only then that Joe dared to clean out the eggshells and tidy up her coop. She had been standing guard, eyeing him

1. Well, all right, her beak.

124

with suspicion and threatening him with low "Auuuuuuuuk's," and he'd been afraid to put his hands near her nest, lest she take one of his fingers off.

By the next day Molly was happily showing her brood all over the place. They explored every corner of the yard. She fussed over them and worried about them and scolded them, and never—not once—let one of them out of her sight. Joe and Grandmother had their eyes on swivels, watching her. And at last they managed to kidnap four of the strongest and fluffiest chicks. Grandmother had a basket ready and Joe plopped them in. She put a napkin over the top, and he made the trek through the streets, down to the shop where he'd stolen the chick so many days ago. Seemed like years, he thought. So much had happened.

And so it was finally finished. He had asked forgiveness for stealing the chick. He had given the shopkeeper back four for one. And he had transferred his sin to Jesus of Nazareth, the Lamb of God.

There was just one problem.

He didn't *feel* anything. Just empty and let down.

He remembered a story Jesus had told once, about a farmer planting his seed. Some of them fell by the wayside and the birds came and ate them. Some of them fell on shallow soil and couldn't grow strong roots—so they grew a little, then withered and died. Some of them fell among thorns and thistles—and they grew a little, and then were choked out. But some of them fell on good soil. And did *they* ever grow, Jesus had said. Nothing could stop them.

Whatever Jesus had planted in *him*, Joe thought, wasn't growing.

And it didn't help to talk about it either.

No matter what he said to Grandmother about Jesus, she could not quite bring herself to believe it.

And Andy thought he had lost his marbles.

The old life at the Temple wasn't fun anymore. It gave him a queasy feeling, a feeling that something was wrong.

So the days went by. Slow and lazy. And dull.

And then the most astonishing rumors began to fly about!

Jesus of Nazareth might be gone—but the stories about Him were flying all over Jerusalem!

125

First the report came that He had begun to appear to the disciples; He had appeared to two of them along the roadside on their way to Emmaus. And He had appeared to the others in an upper room where they were gathered. And yes—He had appeared to them all on the shores of Lake Galilee. He just kept appearing in the most improbable places and in the most astonishing manner.

He walked through locked doors!

And—the rumors went—He had told them that they would have to *continue* the work that He had begun!

Were these things true? Could they be?

Yes!

He had not only talked with them; He had actually *eaten* with them! Hundreds of people had seen Him! And He had hundreds of secret followers!

*Could it be true?*

Andy wouldn't believe it.

And Grandmother thought it was idle gossip.

And after awhile, Joe began to wonder if it was only idle gossip too.

Especially the latest rumor. It was the hardest one to believe. And the hardest one to even *understand.*

He had told His disciples that He would leave them again, to go back to His Father in heaven. But that He would send *another* comforter—THE HOLY SPIRIT—to teach them, and to give them power.

And what's more, they were to wait in Jerusalem until the HOLY SPIRIT came.

THE HOLY SPIRIT!

Who was *He*—THE HOLY SPIRIT?!?

Joe was absolutely befuddled.

"Well these stories can't go on forever," Grandmother said. "Something's either got to happen, or they'll just die down."

By this time nearly six weeks had gone by. Molly's chickens were no longer cute and fluffy. They were tall and gawky now. And they didn't follow her about any more.

Six weeks is a long time.

People paid less and less attention to the rumors.

It looked as if they were what Grandmother had said—idle gossip.

And then came the most astonishing rumor of all.

Jesus had led His disciples up to the Mount of Olives, people said. And He had told them that THE HOLY SPIRIT would come upon them and give them power (there it was again!) to tell everybody everywhere that He had come as the Lamb of God—*and had died on Passover day as a sacrifice for the sins of the people.*

And then, before their very eyes, He had risen into the air, and as they had watched Him, He had disappeared into a cloud!

And they had just stood there, straining their eyes to see the last of Him!

They were absolutely flabbergasted.

But that hadn't been the end of it.

Before they'd been able to gather their wits, two angels had appeared at their sides, and had said, "Why are you staring at the sky? Jesus has gone to heaven. And some day—just as He went—He will return."

And then the angels had disappeared!

The disciples had just stood there staring at each other.

*What now?*

And then they had remembered.

WAIT IN JERUSALEM.

"And did they wait?" said Grandmother, when she heard this bit of gossip in the Temple court. "Are they waiting?"

"Oh, yes!" the people said. "Somewhere in Jerusalem."

But no one knew where.

Well, it did look like the "rumor to end all rumors"—just before the whole thing finally died down.

A day went by.

Nothing happened.

Two days.

Nothing happened.

Three days, four days, five days.

Nothing.

Six days, seven days, eight days—

Nine days—

Ten days. The day of the Feast of the Pentecost!

Uncle Simon had come the night before and stayed over with Joe and Grandmother so he'd be up and ready on the great day.

For the Feast of Pentecost was an important one in the land. Almost as important as the Feast of the Passover. It was, in fact, seven weeks after the Feast of the Passover—a week of weeks! And so it was called the "Feast of Weeks" as well as the Feast of Pentecost. It was the time they celebrated the wheat harvest. And people came to Jerusalem from all over the country to bring their offerings to God and thank Him for their spring crops. Uncle Simon had come alone; Aunt Rachel had stayed behind with the children.

Joe was glad for the excitement. Things had been dull. Andy wasn't fun anymore. And everything that had happened at Passover now seemed somehow like a dream. There were times when Joe wondered if it had *really* happened—if he had really been that close to Jesus that day when Jesus had been on His way to the cross. Or if he had *really* heard his own name. How could anything that had seemed so real, seem so *un*real now?

Joe thought of this as he trotted alongside Uncle Simon on their way to the Temple on Pentecost day. They were walking down the very streets that he had walked down then.

The city was jammed again with worshipers from many nations. And they were jostling and gawking and gossiping—just as they had done then.

Except that Pilate was gone.

And Herod was gone.

And Jesus was gone.

Again, Joe was filled with a great emptiness. He wanted to cling to Uncle Simon's hand. But he felt he was too grown-up.

And then they heard it.

The sound of a mighty roaring wind in the skies!

Were they imagining things?

No!

Other people heard it too. They were looking up. Was it a storm?

No. It was something mysterious they'd never heard before!

128

And then the people, shouting.

"This way!"

"Over this way!"

"What is it?"

"I don't know—it's coming from over this way!"

And then the crowds went apouring into one of the narrow streets, Uncle Simon and Joe along with them—stumbling, tripping over merchandise in front of the shops, catching their balance and stumbling on—

By the time they got to the house where the noise was, the crowds were so thick that Uncle Simon lifted Joe up on a window ledge a few houses away, so he could see.

Joe watched. And listened.

"What is it? What's happened?"

"Don't know. It's over that house."

"It's *in* the house!"

The wind *was* in the house. And what's more—so were the disciples and about a hundred of Jesus' other followers.

But it was not only the wind.

There were what looked like flames or tongues of fire filling the huge upper room, and settling on the heads of everyone there!

The "rumor" about the HOLY SPIRIT was true!

THE HOLY SPIRIT HAD COME!

And the power had come!

For those up close to the house heard the disciples speaking—but not in their own Galilean dialect. They were speaking in the languages and the dialects of the people who were gathered outside!

"How can this be?" the people were asking each other. "What's going on? These men are Galileans. And here we are, from Parthia,

And Elam,

And Media,

And Mesopotamia,

And Judea,

And Cappadocia,

And Phrygia,

129

And Pontus,
And Asia,
And Pamphylia,
And Egypt,
And Libya,
And Rome—"

On and on. They had come to the Feast of Pentecost from just about *everywhere*.

"They're speaking in my language!"
"But I can understand them in *mine!*"
"They are telling of the mighty works of God!"
And then, some smart alecks, "Yaaaa—they're drunk!"
And others took up the cry.
"Haaa! Drunk—drunk—DRUNK!"
Then some of the disciples came out of the house and onto the balcony. One of them raised his hand for silence.

"Listen, all of you!" he cried. "Residents of Jerusalem and visitors alike! ALL of you!"

The crowd grew more quiet.

"Some of you are saying we are drunk. It isn't true. It's only nine o'clock in the morning—too early to be drunk."

Now people were shushing each other, to listen.

"God told you many years ago that He would send the Messiah," the disciple went on, "and He did."

He *did?* People looked at each other. What was coming?

"And when the Messiah came, God let you use the Roman governor to kill Him! But God raised Him from the dead—*as you well know!*"

Silence now, absolute silence.

"For this Messiah is JESUS OF NAZARETH—THE LORD!"
Nobody moved.

"And what you are seeing now was promised centuries ago. God promised that He would pour out His Holy Spirit on believers! And He has! THE HOLY SPIRIT HAS COME!"

Joe's mouth dropped open.

People seemed to be stunned.

And a great sense of awe and wonder came over them.

And then they began to cry out to the disciples—"Brothers! What should we *do?*"

"Each of you must turn back to God," the disciple shot back, "and be baptized in the name of Jesus Christ for the forgiveness of your sins. Then you shall also receive this gift of the Holy Spirit!"

Then he went on to tell them all about Jesus and urging them to turn to Him and be saved.

And then, and then—

Some of them began to work their way through the crowd toward the disciples.

They wanted to accept Jesus of Nazareth as the Son of God—

And as their Saviour!

First a few,

Then dozens of them,

Then hundreds of them,

Then thousands of them.

It was like an enormous worship service, right there on the street.

And then Uncle Simon lifted up his arms and reached behind him for Joe's hands. Joe took Uncle Simon's hands, and slid his legs over Uncle Simon's shoulders. And Uncle Simon moved away from the window ledge, and without a word began to edge his way through the crowd, toward the disciples.

And a strange sense of joy came over Joe, and a strange sense of power filled him.

And this time he knew it was there to stay.

Jesus of Nazareth was the Messiah. He would never doubt it again.

He was grateful to the disciple who had stepped out so boldly to tell the crowd about it. And he strained his eyes to see him better, as Uncle Simon got closer to the house.

And then he realized who it was.

He straightened up a bit on Uncle Simon's shoulders. And his heart leaped for joy.

It was Peter.

---

It was much later in the morning when Joe and Uncle Simon wound their way through the twisting streets, headed for home. The sense of joy was still with Joe, and he knew that Uncle Simon felt it too. They talked softly, closer than they had ever been before.

Their lives would be changed now.

He had to tell Andy, the first chance he got.

But first they had to get home to tell Grandmother.

Their lives would *all* be changed. For Joe had a feeling that this time, she was going to believe it.

He hurried along the street with Uncle Simon.

And then, just for a minute, he turned and walked backward.

So he could see where he had been.